Whistling at Snakes

Grateful acknowledgement is made for permission from the following to reprint material in their control:

"Mama's Banking System," from Mature Living, (date unknown). ©Copyright The Sunday School Board of the Southern Baptist Convention. All rights reserved. Used by permission.

"My Aunt Was a Real Princess," from Mature Living, July 1983. ©Copyright 1983 The Sunday School Board of the Southern Baptist Convention. All rights reserved. Used by permission.

"Bring Them In," from The Church Musician, September 1981. ©Copyright 1981 The Sunday School Board of the Southern Baptist Convention. All rights reserved. Used by permission.

"The Rains Came Down," from The Church Musician, (date unknown). ©Copyright The Sunday School Board of the Southern Baptist Convention. All rights reserved. Used by permission.

Selections from "Minister's Desk" first appeared in the Greenwood Index-Journal. Used by permission.

"What's It Like to Be a Paperboy?" appeared May 16, 1982, in the Greenville News-Piedmont. Used by permission.

"How Great Thou Art" ©Copyright 1953. Renewed 1981 by Manna Music. Used with acknowledgement.

"Let Others See Jesus in You" ©Copyright 1924. Renewed 1952 by Broadman Press. Used with acknowledgement.

"What a Friend We Have in Jesus" Public domain.

Edited and designed by Butch Blume.
Illustrations by Thomas Addison.

Published by COURIERPUBLISHING.

PRINTED IN THE UNITED STATES OF AMERICA.

# Whistling at Snakes

by Horace Sims

# Editor's Note

It is hard to believe that 2014 marks the 15th anniversary of the publication of "Whistling at Snakes" by the late Horace Sims. The response to the original 1999 collection of Sims' work was overwhelming, and the book went through three separate printings.

For several years, long after supplies were depleted, we continued to hear from readers of The Baptist Courier who wanted to purchase a copy of "Whistling at Snakes." Now, to help mark the official launch of CourierPublishing, our book production division, we are happy to re-release this definitive collection of Horace Sims' work.

The edition you are holding includes all of the stories and line drawings from the original book. Also, as a bonus, this 15th-anniversary edition contains 24 new drawings by award-winning artist Thomas Addison, who illustrated the original book.

We think Horace Sims' homespun tales of family, faith and life's unexpected turns have a timeless quality. We invite you to step into a world where a nervous preacher whistles away snakes and decide for yourself.

# Introduction

It is next to impossible not to pick up and thumb through a book with the title of "Whistling At Snakes" and difficult to put it down after sampling the wit and wisdom of The Baptist Courier's late columnist, Horace Sims.

The Courier published the first batch of his short essays, "Horace Sims At Large," in 1997, followed by a second compilation of his columns, "Horace Sims Still At Large," in 1998. Both were timed for distribution at the annual meetings of the South Carolina Baptist Convention in November.

These books, like his "At Large" pieces, achieved immediate and lasting popularity with the Courier's readers. Many turned to his column first before reading anything else in our publication.

Horace always managed to take life seriously while looking at it lightly. He could always find at least a little and often a lot that was funny. And this was so whether the egg was all over his or somebody else's face.

He had no peers as a teller of sidesplitting tales. Some were even true. Asked about that, he explained, "All the stories I've written are based on real events. They tell true happenings." Then, breaking into a smile, he added, "Some of them may have been embellished for the enjoyment of the reader."

It was nearly four years ago that I, as the new editor of The Baptist Courier, sat down to breakfast with Horace at Shoney's in Greenwood with an offer for him to write a regular column that we later named "At Large." His writing, so deceptively simple that many never realized how much work he put into his craft, quickly captured a huge audience that stretched well beyond South Carolina and even the United States. In fact, readers in at least 14 states and 27 foreign countries requested copies of his books.

In November of 1998, the Courier honored Horace at the Abney Memorial Baptist Church in Greenwood, where he had been pastor for nearly three decades, citing his contribution to Christian journalism and South Carolina Baptist life through his column.

Last May, only weeks after his death, the Courier again paid tribute to its former columnist by presenting the first annual Horace B. Sims Jr. Award for academic excellence in the field of Christian studies at North Greenville College. Horace was to have delivered the college's commencement address and receive an honorary doctor of divinity degree, which was awarded posthumously.

Horace held only two pastorates, Abney Memorial and Cayce's Middleton Street Baptist Church, which no longer exists. He graduated from Parker High School in Greenville and attended Furman University. He served a term as president of the South Carolina Baptist Convention in 1982. At the time of his death, he was the convention's parliamentarian and a trustee of Connie Maxwell Children's Home in Greenwood.

He was a regular contributor to the Greenwood Index-Journal newspaper. His writing also appeared in the Greenville News, South Carolina Wildlife magazine, and two Southern Baptist publications: Mature Living and The Church Musician.

This is not the book that the Courier wanted to publish. What we anticipated was to print another installment in a continuing series of column collections in time for release at the November state Baptist convention. But Horace's untimely death broke our hearts and changed our plans. It sadly became necessary to produce a "complete Horace Sims," an anthology of his writings made available for his faithful following.

"Whistling At Snakes," drawn from the title of one of his columns, is the result. In addition to all of the Courier columns that Horace wrote between 1996 and 1999, this book contains some of his articles printed elsewhere, along with material never before published.

In his introduction to "Horace Sims Still At Large," the Courier columnist wrote, "I hope you enjoy reading these stories as much as I have enjoyed writing them." We hope so, too.

Don Kirkland
August 1999

# A Legacy of Laughter

South Carolina Baptists are blessed with a rich history filled with wonderful legacies of those who have gone on before. Men like Richard Furman, John Broadus and Basil Manly left us with great educational legacies. Luther Rice, Janie Chapman and Martha Franks gave their lives to fulfilling the Great Commission, and in doing so left behind terrific missions legacies. We also enjoy historical legacies from some of our founding fathers, such as William Screven, James P. Boyce and Oliver Hart.

I believe Horace Sims left a legacy as well. I, his son, had a tremendous opportunity to get to know this man of diverse interests. He was a parliamentarian, collector, historian, author, humorist, woodcarver, trustee, husband, and a friend. The relationship that I shared with Horace Sims was fourfold in its nature: he was my father, pastor, mentor, and my hero.

As my father, he instilled in me the morals and values that his father instilled in him. He taught me how to fish and to throw a football. He prayed for me, and in doing so taught me how to pray. He loved me and taught me how to love. However, the greatest thing that my father did was lead me to Jesus Christ. He knelt with me in our backyard as the rain began to fall, and I surrendered my life to Jesus.

As my pastor, he was a servant, always putting his sheep before himself. He preached the Word of God with conviction. He preached the Word as our source of truth, and he taught me about the treasures waiting to be found within its pages. He provided wise counsel for every aspect of my life. He fed his Lord's sheep faithfully all the days of his life.

As my mentor, he studied to show himself approved. To say that he loved to read would be a huge understatement. He loved knowledge and kept a constant stream of it flowing into his mind. He taught me that nothing is worth compromising your values or beliefs for. I watched as he showed me time after time that all men are created equal. It didn't matter to him if you were the pastor of the largest church in the convention or the usher at the smallest church; you were equal in the sight of God—and in the eyes of Horace, also.

As my hero, he faced death boldly and courageously, placing himself in the Creator's hands. His faith stood strong through life's toughest trial. He never questioned or complained about the cross he was called to bear, but rather, he lifted it to his shoulder and followed after his Lord.

However, the most important lesson that he ever taught me was how to laugh. I learned from him that laughter can be one of our greatest acts of worship. The foundation of Christian laughter is the joy of our salvation, the variety and creativity of God's creation, the blessings that He bestowed upon our lives, and the blessed promises of His Word. That is what enabled my father to laugh as he walked through the valley of the shadow of death. For, you see, the source of his laughter was "the peace that passeth understanding." Take this book, put aside all of your stress, worry or sorrow, and laugh—for the legacy that Horace Sims left us was laughter.

H. Bryant Sims III
July 1999

# Whistling
## at
# Snakes

*I am grateful for the memories that linger—the big radio, the sandwich by the bed at night—and especially for the memory of my granny who smoked a pipe.*

*Horace Sims*

# SECTION ONE

# At Large

Columns originally
published in
The Baptist Courier
1996–1999

# Whistling at Snakes

Every time I go to the Lowcountry to speak, I hear a lot of stories about snakes. I am told that snakes will not hurt you. But I am one who believes snakes can make you hurt yourself.

At one church, I was told that a rattlesnake had been killed in the hall of the church. Another one had been killed in the guest bedroom of the parsonage. I really wanted to sleep in my car.

I took a minister from Maine to speak at a small membership church conference in the Lowcountry. When we got to the church, he saw a piece of rope under a tree and would not get out of the car until I picked it up.

I returned to that church to speak in revival services. I was not excited about going to "rattlesnake kingdom." One of the deacons in my church told me to whistle a lot. He said whistling would scare away snakes.

So I got out of my car, whistling. I whistled all the way to the church. I whistled all the way to the parsonage. Everywhere I went, I whistled. I whistled hymns, I whistled marches, I whistled jazz. I whistled everything I thought a snake would not like.

The pastor finally said, "You sure do like to whistle, don't you?"

I said, "I'm keeping snakes away."

"Keeping snakes away?" he asked.

"Yeah, and I'm doing a good job, because I haven't seen one yet,"

I replied.

He said, "That could be, but this is not really snake season."

## Big Bubba

I had been asked to preach in revival services at a small church within driving distance from my home. I made the trip of about 60 miles each night for a week.

The pastor of the church was an old friend of many years. I enjoyed his company each night. He had told me the church could not pay an honorarium, but would take a love offering. Since money has never been a major object to me, I agreed to this arrangement.

The services went well. The music was good. The preaching wasn't too bad. The church was faithful to its promise in taking a love

offering each night. After the service, one of the ushers would empty the offering plate into my coat pocket. When I got home, I would count the offering.

The offering amount ranged from $9 to $12. One night, I received $13. To tell the truth, that was probably more than the sermons were worth.

When I arrived at the church on the last night, there was a small camper parked right out front. A hand-lettered sign read, "Little Suzy, The Gospel Singing Wonder." She was to furnish the special music for the service. Little Suzy sang to the top of her voice. She was accompanied on guitar by her parents.

When Little Suzy completed her concert, the pastor announced a love offering for her. The offering was taken, and Little Suzy got $32.50.

I felt a rise of excitement within myself. This could be the night for a good love offering. The pastor called for a love offering for "this man of God who has been so faithful to come each evening with a message from the Lord." When I got home and counted my offering, I had received $11.18.

I told my wife that I was going to change careers. I was going to get a guitar and a camper and call myself "Big Bubba, The Gospel Singing Marvel."

## Lightning Strikes

I was elected as a deacon in my home church when I was 23 years old and single. This caused a small stir among the people. Some said that the Bible taught that a deacon was to be the husband of one wife. Others said the Bible taught that a deacon could not have two living wives. While they quietly discussed this issue, I was elected chairman of the deacons.

The work of the deacon is very important to the church. They are

to be ministers to the needs of the church family. I always enjoyed being a deacon, wife or not.

Being a deacon can be a dangerous job. I experienced my most dangerous deacons meeting after becoming a pastor. We had met to discuss the church custodian. Some felt that he was not doing the job right and should be replaced.

While we were meeting, a very strong thunderstorm came up. The wind was strong and the lightning was furious. Just as a motion was made to seek a new custodian, the lightning struck the steeple of the church.

Now, the deacons were meeting in a room directly beneath the steeple. There was a great explosion in the room. Balls of fire went in all directions. Deacons were knocked from their chairs. A light switch flew out of the wall and struck me in the back of the head. I fell from my seat on top of the chairman, who was already on the floor. He hasn't walked exactly right since.

Our steeple was destroyed. A large hole was knocked in the roof. The fire department came to check for fire. The evening service was canceled.

Two decisions were made at the next deacons meeting. The custodian was given a raise and a new contract. Some felt that it was possible that he had better connections than the pastor and deacons did. The deacons also decided to meet in a different room each month, so as not to be such a good target for the lightning.

## View From the Balcony

My home church had a balcony that went around the sanctuary. This was the place all of us boys wanted to sit. But Mama would not allow it. We sat on the Sims pew, third row from the back left.

On some Sundays, Mama had to help keep the nursery. On those mornings, Daddy would sit in the balcony. We could sit there if our

dad did. There would be a long row of dads, all asleep. We boys were free in the balcony.

Things look different from the balcony. Bald heads looked like melons in a melon patch. There were all sizes and shapes. The ripest were surrounded by gray grass.

You could see how many people took their shoes off during the service. You could see how many of the ladies in the choir were reading magazines while the preacher was waxing eloquent.

The balcony was also a good place to spy on the courting couples on the back row. You could see who was holding hands with whom. You could also see if they were playing "footsie" during a good sermon on hell.

The Bible talks about a great cloud of witnesses looking down on us from heaven. I know the Lord looks down on us from the balcony of heaven. He sees us as we are—bald heads, bare feet, hand-holders and all.

## Names

"A name is a name unless it is the same." This is not a quotation from Shakespeare. It is a quotation from Sims.

My dad was Horace Bryant Sims, Sr. He named me Horace Bryant Sims, Jr. That's where all the confusion began. I always got mistaken for my dad.

While a student at Furman University, I worked at the same plant with my father. We even worked in the same department together. We always answered the same call, so the men named me "Junior." For several years, I was known as Junior Sims. In fact, those men still call me that when I happen to see one of them.

My dad was in the class of 1933 at Furman. I was in the class of 1962. Even though I wasn't born until 1940, I received alumni mail for the class of '33. Dad got the mail for '62.

When Dad died a few years ago, I stopped getting any alumni mail. I guess Furman has me listed as being among the dead. I wish the IRS would make the same mistake.

When my son was born, I took one look at him and told my wife we would name him Horace Bryant Sims, III. We decided to call him Bryant instead of Horace. When he got to high school, he was called by his first name, Horace. He finally got people to just call him H.B.

Well, things went along all right until he got married, and we tried to change his car insurance. My daughter-in-law called the other day and told me their new policy was made out to Horace B. Sims, Jr., and wife Melanie Knowles Sims. My wife looked at our policy and it was made out to Horace B. Sims, Jr., and wife Jane B. Sims.

Now, look at the mess I'm in. If I have a wreck and they check my insurance, I could be charged with bigamy. I guess I should take the name that was on a recent letter. It was addressed to Horace B. Sin, Ellendrug Avenue.

## Swatty Wasp

A wasp, according to Webster's Collegiate Dictionary, is a "solitary, winged, hymenopterous insect with an often formidable sting."

It could also be said: "An insect that adds life and excitement to an otherwise dull Sunday morning worship service."

We boys always rushed to the sanctuary after Sunday school so we could get the funeral home fans that were not broken in the middle. These fans made great wasp swats. When a wasp flew by close enough, you could send him into a completely out-of-control flight with just one swat.

I remember hitting a wasp with a good, sound lick. He flew out of control for about three pews and into a lady's bouffant. She jumped to her feet and ran out of the church in the middle of the choir special. I would rather have a wasp in my bouffant than what I got when I got home.

On a hot Sunday morning, one of the deacons was sitting in the middle of one of the longest pews. He suddenly jumped to his feet, clutching his pants leg, and said, "I've got him! I've got the rascal!" He crawled over everybody in the pew and then rushed to the vestibule, still clutching his pants leg. In the vestibule, he dropped his pants and set the wasp free.

Now, our music director gave us some advice. He told us to leave the wasps alone and they would leave us alone. The pastor then rose to read the morning scripture. As he read, a wasp flew between him and his Bible. The wasp made several return trips, disrupting the pastor from his reading each time. The pastor finally laid his Bible down and said, "Brother choir director, that was good advice that you gave us. The good Lord knows that I have tried to follow it, but I'm putting this wasp on notice. If he flies between me and my Bible one more time, I'm gonna belt the devil out of him right here on the pulpit."

At last, the pastor was on our side, and we boys were saying under our breath, "Go, man, go."

## Chrome Dome

I've heard it all:

"God only made so many perfect heads—all the rest he covered with hair."

"Hair and brains don't mix. Which did you lose first?"

"Hey, Chrome Dome, is that you?"

One advertising jingle read, "'I use it, too,' the bald man said. 'It keeps my face just like my head. Burma Shave!'"

It may surprise you to know that I once had a full head of kinky hair. Mama would get the comb caught in the kinks while getting me ready for school. I used to say, "I wish God had made me baldheaded." No one had told me that God listened to children. I can imagine

God saying to me, "All right, big boy, is there anything else you wish I had done differently?"

You may not believe this, either: I did have to go to the barber-shop when I was young. It was old-fashioned; you had to sit and wait your turn. Daddy always took us on Saturday. That was the most interesting day of the week. The men from the mills would come by to get all spruced up for the weekend. They would bring a change of clothes so they could take a shower. They would also get a shave, a haircut, and a shoeshine.

The old shop smelled of lilac water aftershave, talcum powder, and cigars. The talk was about hunting, fishing, and whatever had taken place in the mill that week. There was always a game of checkers, using bottle caps, being played in the corner. Someone was always waiting to play the winner.

The older barber was the one who cut my hair. On the wall behind his chair was a little sign painted with glitter, which read: "Only one life will soon be past, only what's done for Christ will last."

That little sign in that old-fashioned barbershop became the driving force in my life and in my ministry.

It is true. Little things do count.

# Holy Laughter

When I was a boy, we didn't own a motor vehicle of any kind. We rode the electric trolley or the bus. We also did a lot of walking.

When we went to my aunt's home in the summer, we would ride the trolley to West Greenville and then catch the bus that ran from Greenville to Clemson. We went through many small towns until we arrived in Central. My uncle would be waiting there to take us to their home near Six Mile.

My aunt and uncle lived in a large, two-story house on top of a hill. My uncle was a stone mason and built his own house.

We were city boys, and a visit to the country was always exciting to us. We were also straight-laced Southern Baptist boys. There was nothing charismatic about our church. We only sang songs out of the Broadman Hymnal. Our music was played on a piano and an organ. We did not know anything about canned music.

Now, my aunt and uncle belonged to a different denomination. They were not Baptist. Their church was charismatic. Their worship was completely different from ours back home. The preacher ran up and down the aisle, preaching and shouting. The people shouted in response.

We straight-laced Southern Baptist boys were petrified. Out of sheer fear, we began to laugh. My aunt would take us outside and tell us to stay there until we quit laughing. I pointed out that some of the men in the church were laughing. My aunt said that was a holy laugh.

It took me a long time to understand that. Psychologists tell us that we laugh at the ludicrous, the incongruous, the ridiculous, the contradictory, and in response to the comedic in life. They never mention holy laughter.

Well, it's like this. When God does an absolutely stupendous miracle in your life, and you are so overwhelmed with joy that you want to run out into the field and lift your head heavenward, and burst into a laugh of joy and thanksgiving, my aunt would have called that a holy laugh.

And I wouldn't want to miss that for anything in the world.

# Faulty Zipper

I grew up on the mill-village side of town. I attended a large church, but it was not a big downtown church. My first job was delivering the afternoon newspaper downtown. To get there, I had to ride the electric trolley. On the way, I would pass one of the big downtown churches.

This church had some great preachers. I would listen to them on their Sunday afternoon radio broadcasts. I always wondered what it would be like to attend worship services in that big church. I even wondered what it would be like to preach there.

Well, as time went on, I felt called to the ministry myself. My first church was a small-size church in the mid-state. My second church was a medium-size church. I have been pastor there for over 25 years. I have never been pastor of a big downtown church.

A few years ago, the pastor of that big downtown church I had passed on the trolley invited me to preach on a Sunday morning. I was totally excited. I called my mama. She said, "Act like you have got good sense." My wife said I should get a new suit. I went to the local discount outlet clothing store to get a new suit. I bought a ninety-nine-dollar, navy blue, polyester suit. I even bought a four-dollar tie to match. I was ready to make my appearance at the downtown church.

The big day came. I marched onto the platform with the pastor. The pipe organ was at full throttle. The choir sang a glorious anthem. The buttons on my shirt were stressed by the prideful swell of my chest. I could just imagine the next day's headlines, "Mill Village Boy Preaches at Big Downtown Church."

After the prayer, I took my seat on the platform pew. It was then I experienced the platform speaker's nightmare. There was a popping sound and a rush of cold air. The zipper on the fly of my new, ninety-nine-dollar, navy blue, polyester suit had burst open.

Sweat popped out on my head. My heart felt faint. My breathing became labored. Then I had a calming thought. I wondered how many of the great preachers who had preached from that pulpit had done so with their flies standing open. I may have made history that day. But I was glad that I didn't make the headlines.

## Crown of Flowers

In "Canterbury Tales," Chaucer described the son of the knight as "embroidered like a meadow bright and full of freshest flowers, red and white. Singing he was, or fluting all the day."

Now, you have to understand this classical stuff from your own native environment. Chaucer came to life in a Sunday morning worship service back home.

My home church was one of the first in our part of town to air-condition the sanctuary. It was a great and historic day when the air was turned on for the first time. People came from all around just to sit in a church with air-conditioning.

Our sanctuary was always decorated with a metal, fan-shaped basket of fresh-cut gladiolus. These were always placed on the window sill of the baptistry, just above the choir.

When the air conditioner came on, it drew the drapes back into the baptistry. When it shut off, the drapes returned to their normal position. In returning, they nudged the flower basket off of the window sill. The basket capped one of the men in the choir just like a baseball cap. There he stood in his choir robe, "embroidered like a meadow bright and full of freshest flowers, red and white." He pulled the flowers from in front of his face and asked, "Pastor, may I be excused?" He left the choir with his new floral crown still in place.

I tell you, Chaucer was never more real or exciting.

## Missing Old Times

I guess I am from the old school. There are just some things I miss in the church services. I miss a sanctuary with a wrap-around balcony. We boys loved to launch a paper airplane attack from there at the end of the morning service.

I miss the old hymns accompanied by a piano and an organ. I just don't relate to a lot of modern music.

I miss funeral home fans. They added a certain swaying motion to the congregation. Not only were they good for swatting wasps, you could also swat your brother if he sat too close to you on the pew.

And I miss women's hats. I think I'll start a movement to encourage women to wear hats to church. My mama never looked better than when she wore her Sunday hat.

Back at my home church, we had a lady who wore a hat with a brim that was at least three feet in diameter. She was always five minutes late for service. She would sashay down the aisle to the second pew from the front. The brim of the hat would rise and fall with each step. To us boys, it looked like a flying saucer coming in for a landing.

My favorite hat was worn by a lady in the choir. It was covered with peacock feathers. As she sang, she kept beat to the music by shaking her head. The feathers looked like a hundred eyeballs above the choir.

Come on, ladies, wear the hats again.

## Stage Fright

Stage fright is that nervousness felt at appearing before an audience. Its symptoms are shortness of breath, sweating of the palms, and perspiration that runs down the back of your legs and puddles in your shoes.

I remember that the purpose of Baptist Training Union was to train us to stand up before a group and speak. Well, I went to BTU for years, and I still get stage fright. I pace back and forth in the hall each Sunday morning, getting ready to go to the pulpit.

It started in high school. I played in the band. There were about 150 of us. We all dressed in the same uniforms and wore white shoes.

The first time we marched onto the football field, I could hardly get enough breath to play my clarinet. I just knew every eye was on me.

At my home church, the deacon chairman conducted the business conference. My first time, I stopped at the water fountain for some water. I caught my tie tack on the fountain and broke my clip-on tie. I had to go tie-less to the conference. I felt like I was falling backward and pulling the pulpit over on me.

My speech teacher in college said it was all right for your knees to knock. It was when they missed that you should sit down quickly. After speaking to groups of all kinds and sizes for more than 30 years, my knees still knock. Once or twice, I believe they came close to missing.

## WMU Fireworks

I grew up in a poor family by today's standards. Our house was a typical mill community house. It did not have sub-flooring or underpinning. The cold winter winds would blow through the cracks in the floor and make the linoleum rug hum around the edges. All of the rooms, except the dining room, were heated by open fireplaces. The dining room had a Warm Morning heater.

We did have electricity. Each room had one electric cord hanging from the ceiling, with a socket and a light bulb at the end. The living room and the dining room each had one wall plug-in.

When company came, Mama had a table lamp she would use for light. This was fancier than the ceiling cord.

Well, Mama's WMU circle gathered in the dining room for a meeting. Mama had removed the light bulb from the ceiling socket to put in her table lamp. The ladies were discussing missions, among other things. The pound cake was ready for refreshments. Coffee and tea were on the table. The ladies' minds were not on the boys playing in the bedroom across the hall.

My younger brother was always mechanically inclined. He took a box of paper clips and hooked them together end to end and made a chain.

While the WMU ladies were in deep prayer and meditation, he slipped across the hall to the dining room. He climbed up on the dining room table and inserted the paper clips in the open light socket.

Great balls of fire filled the dining room. The WMU ladies, including Mama, ran screaming from the house. My brother was doing a fancy version of the jitterbug on top of the table. My aunt took the broom and knocked him from the table on her way out of the house.

The WMU ladies never came back to our house. Mama was humiliated. She told Daddy all about it when he got home.

My brother and I could never convince Daddy that paper clips, light sockets, and great balls of fire had anything at all to do with the study of missions.

He did, however, convince us that we shouldn't ever try to mix the two again.

## Taxi Ride

I love to travel. I like staying in big hotels and riding in taxicabs. We flew to Los Angeles to attend the Southern Baptist Convention. We stayed at the big Bonaventure Hotel in downtown Los Angeles. This hotel consists of five tall glass towers. A lot of movies and television shows are filmed there. We South Carolina preachers were in high cotton.

On our last day there, the travel host gave me $25 for taxi fare. He told me to take five of my friends and meet him at the Biltmore Hotel, where we would board a bus for the airport.

We crowded ourselves into a cab and were soon speeding over the streets of Los Angeles. The driver turned into the Third Street tunnel. He was going the wrong way on a one-way street. I was seated in the front. All I could get out was, "One way, one way."

The driver smiled and said in very bad English, "Yes, I go one way."

I shouted back, "Wrong way, wrong way."

He repeated, "Yes, I go one way."

We came out of the tunnel alive only by the grace of God. The other five men were so quiet, I thought they had died of heart failure.

We raced up and down the back streets of Los Angeles. The driver stopped at a hotel that men of God had no business being at. He said, "This is Baltimore Hotel."

I said, "We want the Biltmore Hotel." He raced off again.

He brought us to the Baltimore Hotel four times. I saw a policeman looking at us with great concern. I asked the driver to ask him the way to the Biltmore. He gave the driver directions, and we soon arrived. We had been in the cab a little over an hour.

We grabbed our bags and rushed through the Biltmore Hotel to the waiting bus. As we reached the bus, we were stopped in our tracks. Directly across the street from the Biltmore Hotel was the Bonaventure Hotel that we had left over an hour before.

The ride to the airport was not nearly as exciting.

## Orange Slice Candy

There are some things I have a deep love for. I love orange slice candy. I can resist all other candies except orange slice candy. My love for orange slice candy goes back to my childhood. We rode the trolley from the mill village to downtown every Friday night. We spent most

of our time in the dime stores. Each one of them had a candy counter. Mama bought the same thing every Friday night. She bought Fig Newtons, Spanish peanuts, chocolate drops and orange slice candy.

We knew Mama had a special use for orange slice candy. She would put it up and give us two slices after each dose of castor oil. I don't remember what the castor oil was for, but I do remember how sweet the orange slice candy tasted after a dose of it.

Every time I pass a candy counter, I have to get a bag of orange slice candy. It always reminds me of the castor oil. It also reminds me that the good comes after the bad.

There is something better than orange slice candy. It is the love and forgiveness of our Lord when we've done wrong. He takes the bitterness out of life and fills it with sweetness.

Try his remedy; you'll like it.

## Stranded Missionary

We were excited to have a well-known Baptist missionary visit our church. He was to come on a Wednesday night. I had invited him to spend the night with us. He said he could not because of a speaking engagement the next day.

He arrived on time. He talked to us about Baptist missions work in Nigeria, Africa. The people were very attentive to his talk. He used some artifacts from Africa to make his talk even more interesting.

While he was talking, I could hear a light rain striking the windows. The sound grew louder. It began to sound like sleet. The weather man had not predicted any freezing weather for that night. When we went outside, the ground was covered with ice, and snow had begun to fall.

The missionary took one look and said, "I think I will spend the night." He reminded us that he had been in Africa for over 25 years and had not driven in much snow and ice. He carried one change of clothes for just such an emergency.

By morning we had over a foot of snow. Our guest was stranded. We were just a young couple and were not used to having overnight guests, especially a missionary from Africa.

The snow froze solid. The roads were closed. Our missionary was worried about getting home. He called and canceled his next speaking engagement. We were worried about running out of food. I think our missionary was thinking about the same thing.

He looked out the window and noticed that our neighbor still had collards in his garden. They were sticking up through the snow. Our missionary said he sure would like to have some fresh collards. I called our neighbor and explained our position to him. He said we could have all the collards we wanted, only we would have to go to the garden and cut them. We had several meals of fresh collards.

By Saturday afternoon, the snow was melting and our missionary was able to leave for home. He waved over the top of his car as he rounded the corner.

An unexpected snowstorm brought us a real blessing. I don't think we have had such an interesting house guest since. And besides, we learned a whole lot about Nigeria, Africa.

## Baptismal Shower Cap

A baptismal service can always be an exciting time. Our baptistry consists of a copper tub built over a wooden frame. The steps leading down into the baptistry are also wooden. The very first time I used it, the bottom step came loose and floated to the top of the water. I thought it was some kind of animal and almost yelled, "Every man for himself! I'm going over the glass!"

I had one candidate who asked to be allowed to wear a shower cap. She had a strange hair condition of some kind. After some thought, I consented to let her wear the cap. My wife says what happened after

that was my fault. She said that I did not know the difference between a shower cap and a swimming cap.

I took my place in the baptistry. I was dressed in my white robe and waders. I stood in front of the baptistry window with my hands folded across my chest in the proper ministerial position.

I looked to my deacon assistant at the top of the steps for the next candidate. He looked to his left and looked back at me with a terrible expression on his face. I thought he was having a heart attack. He looked left once again and grimaced in pain.

The deacon stretched his hand out to his left and brought the next candidate to the entrance of the baptistry. This time, I grimaced in pain. She had on a shower cap that looked like the bonnet of a portable hair dryer. It was white with bright orange roses on it. It rose to a point above her head. As I brought her before the baptistry window, a wave of laughter went over the congregation.

When I tried to baptize her, the cap changed its function. It was filled with air and became a life preserver. The further I took her under water, the more her head came to her chest. Realizing the possibility of breaking her neck, I never put her head all the way under.

Looking back over the whole experience, I think I can understand why she never came back.

## Flying Dog

Have you ever seen a flying dog? Well, I have—once.

It happened just this way. My home church had a beautiful old sanctuary. The pews were in a semi-circle around the pulpit area. It had a balcony that completely circled the sanctuary. There were exposed beams in the ceiling. The steps to the balcony went up from the vestibule. With the doors to the sanctuary shut, no one could see who was in the vestibule.

Now, on a Sunday night, the pastor was all involved in the preaching of his sermon. A little boy had taken his seat on the front pew to the left of the pulpit. Unknown to those in the sanctuary, the boy's dog entered the vestibule. Unable to get to the sanctuary, he went to the balcony. He looked through the balcony rail and saw the boy on the front seat.

The dog leaped to the top rail and over he came. His flight took him from the balcony rail to the pulpit, just behind the pastor. The dog howled; the preacher yelled, "Git, git, git that dog outta here!" The old ladies lost their teeth; the old men flipped their wigs; and we kids rolled in the aisles with "holy laughter."

After all, a worship service should be exciting.

# Arrested

It was a beautiful day. The air was filled with excitement. The giant Boeing 747 Air France plane was approaching the Ben-Gurion Airport in Tel-Aviv, Israel. The blue Mediterranean Sea lay beneath us. The pilot announced that we would soon be in Israel.

It was a trip of a lifetime for a preacher. I was soon to be in the land of the Bible. I was going to walk where Jesus walked. I was going to see the Jordan River and the Sea of Galilee. I was going to stand at the top of the Mount of Olives and look down on the old, walled city of Jerusalem.

Well, our plane was soon on the ground in Israel. I had never been so far from home. We were told to remain in our seats until we had been cleared to get off the plane. Israeli military men came on board and looked us over. There was a group of priests from some eastern cult on board. The military guard said they could not get off in Israel. The rest of us were cleared to deplane. I was filled with excitement as I descended the ramp.

Large buses had arrived to take us to the terminal. As I started to get on the bus, a female soldier asked me to follow her. I thought she meant to the back door of the bus. I was met there by a male soldier who nudged me in the back with a machine gun and pointed me toward a small van parked beside the plane. I knew that at any minute I could have more holes in me than a salt shaker. So I went to the van.

I got into the van, where I met another military man seated at a small desk. He had two large stacks of notebooks on the desk. He began to interrogate me. He wanted to know what I had brought to Israel. He wanted to know who I had come to see. I assured him my church had given me the trip as a gift.

After a short time, he stood and smiled, and told the soldier to take me back to the bus. No one ever gave me an explanation. When I got home, one of my friends said it was simple. He said, "They looked at you and said, 'Yessir, you-ara-fat.'"

## Revival Sermons

The preaching of a sermon takes careful planning. It should not be directed at any one person, nor should it be changed because of any one person. Above all, the preacher should know his scripture well enough to get his facts straight.

A friend of mine was preaching a sermon from the account of Noah and the Ark. In the midst of the fury of his preaching, he could not think of the name of Noah. In desperation, he asked, "And who was it that built the ark?"

A little boy sitting near the front said, "Noah."

"That's right, praise God. Even this child knows that it was Noah," said the preacher.

I was speaking in revival services and preached a sermon on Ahab and Jezebel. I titled the sermon "The Danger of Illegitimate Desire."

I said that Ahab and Jezebel were two of the most evil people in the Bible. Their very names brought to mind the thought of evil. The only other person named Ahab that I could think of was the evil captain of Moby Dick. I told the congregation that parents would not name children such despicable names.

After the service, an elderly gentleman came to me and said he really enjoyed the sermon. "My name is Will Jones," he said.

"Thank you for your words of encouragement," I said.

"My name is Will A. Jones," he said.

"I guess that 'A' stands for Ahab," I replied.

"One of those despicable names," he said.

Well, I retired that sermon that night, never to be preached again.

## Highway to Heaven

Someone has said that a sermon is "something that a preacher will cross the country to deliver, but won't cross the street to hear." I have heard one or two that I would cross the street to hear again. One of those is as follows:

The preacher titled his sermon, "The Highway to Heaven." He

began: "Last night I was reading a book on astronomy. I read where it said that there is a vacuum above the North Pole. They ain't no stars, or planets, or anything there. It's just a vacuum. Then I remembered reading that when Satan went up before God, that God's throne was on the side of the North. I put two and two together. That vacuum is the 'Highway to Heaven.'

"Now, I figure that it works like this. It don't matter where a soul dies. It can die in America, or Africa, or Japan, or China, or Australia, or at the South Pole. When that soul dies, it circles the earth till it comes to the North Pole, and there it zooms off to heaven. Now, brothers, I didn't git this sermon out of no book like the rest of these preachers. I figgered this one out for myself."

Well, I have often thought I would go across the street to hear this sermon one more time if I could, but the soul of the preacher has already taken its journey on the "Highway to Heaven."

# Words

We live in a world of words. This is how we communicate. This newspaper is a collection of words. I make my living by speaking and writing words. Public speakers should practice using "right words." Preachers are among those who should make sure they use "right words."

I recently heard a preacher say that Jesus was the personification of his Father. A person can only personify an abstract quality such as love, kindness, gentleness, or goodness. You cannot personify another person. God the Father is a person.

Another word heard a lot is the word "pastored." A preacher said, "I pastored my church for 20 years." The word "pastor" is a noun, not a verb. The correct sentence would be, "I served as pastor of my church for 20 years."

Now, how about the word "borned"? There is no such word. We

are born again. We are not borned again. I hear more and more preachers using the word "borned."

It seems to me we need to return to our blackboards and diagram sentences and conjugate verbs. The teacher in my high school English class asked one of my mill hill friends to conjugate the verb "throw." He stood and said, "Throw, threw, throwed."

After turning several shades of red, she asked another of my friends what was wrong with the word "throwed."

He stood and said, "They ain't no sech word as 'throwed'."

That's a true story, 'cause I was there and seen him when he done it.

## Welcome, Senior Citizen

It hit me like a ton of bricks. I was really minding my own business. I went to a local fast-food restaurant to get my morning biscuit and coffee. The waitress filled my order and then asked "You do get the senior citizen discount, don't you?"

My first reaction was to ask, "Are you crazy?" Then I saw the new, little sign on the wall which read, "Senior citizen discounts begin at 55 years old." Hey, I was two years beyond that.

My biscuit was not quite as good that morning. I guess it was the sudden news that I qualified for a discount. I thought you became a senior citizen when you reached 80 years old, not 55. Who changed the rules? Who had given this young waitress the right to tell me I was now a senior citizen?

I should have taken notice of the signs. Those brown spots on the back of my hands. I had heard my mother and friends talk about those age spots. I did order my new glasses with progressive ground lenses

so the trifocals would not show.

I have noticed that I get winded on long walks. I do try to miss as many steps as possible. I wear special insoles in my shoes. And I can't remember things too well. Lately, I have been given the handicapped room at White Oak Conference Center. I was introduced to a group the other day as one of South Carolina Baptists' senior pastors. But did this give this young waitress the right to hit me so hard with her question?

Well, I went back home and sat down in my favorite recliner and mulled all this over in my mind. I thought about how fast life had gone by. I seemed to have dozed off as I meditated on these things. When I awoke, I decided to put all of this out of my mind.

I went to the mailbox to get the mail. And there it was, lying right on top of the mail—my membership card to the AARP.

## Overflowing Baptistry

We decided to build a social hall at the church. There are a lot of plans that have to be made for such an undertaking. Blueprints have to be drawn. Power and water supplies have to be studied. The site has to be prepared and a foundation laid.

It was determined that our water supply was not good enough to supply a new building adequately. The size of our water pipeline need-ed to be enlarged. We decided to increase the entire line so that we would have better pressure in each of our buildings.

We now had plenty of water. Since the pressure was greater, there had to be some adjustments made at certain outlets. This was a lesson that I was soon to learn.

I turned the water on to fill the baptistry. It usually took about three-and-a-half hours. I went downtown to take care of some busi-ness. I made sure to keep close watch on the time.

When I returned to the church, I could hear a splashing in the baptistry. I thought an animal of some kind must have fallen in. I rushed to the sanctuary to find the water coming over the baptistry glass in waves. The new water line had cut the fill time by 45 minutes.

I had baptized the entire choir loft, carpet, seats and all. I worked the rest of the day, trying to get it dry before the next day.

Some Sundays, sitting on the platform, I still seem to catch the odor of wet, musty carpet.

## First Funeral

Some things you just learn as you go along. There are no classes on how to baptize or on how to conduct a funeral. You can practice baptism on your friends, but not many of them will let you practice burying them.

My first funeral took place on the second day of my first pastorate. I didn't know the deceased. All of her family were from out of state. She was not a member of the church, but had attended there some before going to a nursing home.

The funeral was to be at a country cemetery a few miles out of town. One of the men in the church had volunteered to drive me to the cemetery, since I had no idea where it was.

Just as we arrived at the cemetery, I noticed some commotion in one of the family cars. One of the women said, "You can't bury her there, that's my grave." It seems there had been a mix-up in initials and the funeral home had opened the wrong grave.

The mortician came to me and asked, "Reverend, what are we going to do?" I replied, "This is my first funeral." I had only been a pallbearer once. I had never conducted a funeral, and at that moment I thought I might never do this again.

I saw the backhoe parked in the woods behind the cemetery. I asked the mortician how long it would take to open the right grave. He said, "About 45 minutes." I suggested that we have the graveside service at the place already prepared. He could then ride the people around in the family car while he buried the woman in the right grave. This seemed to suit everybody.

As soon as the graveside service was completed, my driver and I made a beeline home. I spent the next day pondering my decision to preach and bury the dead.

That was 29 years ago. I have preached hundreds of sermons and buried a lot of the dead. And sometimes today, when things haven't gone right, I'm tempted to ponder it all over again.

## Traveling Music

Music is the greatest mover of emotions. Music either calms and soothes, or it excites and moves. A good church music director knows this and can effectively use music to set the tone of the worship service.

Some songs just don't fit the situation. "In the Hour of Trial" just doesn't seem like a good offertory hymn. Nor does "The Fight is On"

go well at a wedding. Or how about "Rise Up O Men of God" at a funeral?

My family has long ago selected some songs as riding songs. We sing them when we are making a trip in the car. They are good old gospel songs that help keep everyone awake.

We like to sing "I'll Fly Away," "A New Name in Glory" and "Kneel at the Cross." I suppose our favorite riding song is Albert E. Brumley's great old gospel song, "I'll Fly Away." It's a real good traveling song.

We were driving back from Calabash, North Carolina, to Sunset Beach by way of a back road. The old station wagon was packed full of family and our children's friends. We were all singing "I'll Fly Away." The road made a 90-degree turn to the left. I could see a red, blinking light just ahead.

I suddenly realized we had missed the turn and were looking at a channel marker in the Intracoastal Waterway.

The old wagon screeched to a stop about a foot from the water. There was absolute silence. Then, one small voice said, "Boy, we almost did fly away."

## Preacher's Special

My doctor says I need to lose weight. He said that I was a little overweight. I always told people that I was just big boned. My doctor says bones don't come that big.

I thought the dry cleaners had shrunk my suit and my blazer. I knew that they stopped meeting. I started wearing wide ties so no one would notice the gap.

I owe a lot of my size to senior citizens. I speak to senior citizen groups just about every week. The pay is not much, but the food is great. They season their food the old way. Nobody can make better fried apple pies and coconut cakes. It is just like at home with Mama.

I was speaking in revival services at a lowcountry church. They announced the church-wide supper on Wednesday night would be "preacher's special." I asked the guest music director if he had ordered us two preacher's specials for Wednesday night. He said he had already taken care of that.

When we arrived at the social hall, they set before us two whole, deep-fried chickens. After a good laugh, they took them away and brought us a regular meal.

After the service, we got in our car to go back to the inn where we were staying. There was a brown bag in the front floor of the car. You guessed it: two whole, deep-fried chickens. We spent half the night eating chicken.

## Welcome to L.A.

Attending the Southern Baptist Convention meetings has always produced some fun experiences. Such was the case in Los Angeles,

California.

I saw an advertisement on television which proclaimed that the best Mexican food in Los Angeles was to be found at the El Pasero Restaurant on Olvera Street. I put that on my list of things to do while in L.A.

I got together a group of Baptist preachers from South Carolina to go with me to El Pasero. We took a cab from our hotel in downtown Los Angeles to Olvera Street.

Now, a cab ride in Greenwood, South Carolina, and a cab ride in Los Angeles, California, are two different things entirely. By the time we got to Olvera Street, there were five Baptist preachers from South Carolina who were prayed up for three weeks in advance.

It didn't take us long to locate the restaurant once we got to Olvera Street. The advertisement on the television was not wrong. We had a Mexican feast. Even the one man who vowed not to eat Mexican food enjoyed it.

When we were ready to leave, the cashier told us to walk to the end of the street, where we would find a bus stop. There would be a shuttle bus to take us back to our hotel.

As we waited for the shuttle, a man seated on the curb got up and came to us. He was highly inebriated.

"May I welcome you good gentlemen to Los Angeles," he said. He looked at me and asked, "What do you do, my good man?"

"I'm a Baptist preacher," I told him.

He asked each one of us the same question and got the same answer. He looked us over very slowly while straightening his coat and cocking his hat to one side. "You might say I have got myself in a most revolting situation," he said. He returned to his seat on the curb.

As we boarded the shuttle for downtown, I wasn't sure we were welcome in Los Angeles.

# A Lot of Water

I had been invited to speak for three nights at the Martha Franks Retirement Home. They were having a mini-version of the state senior adult convention.

A visit to Martha Franks is like a visit to the "Who's Who" of Baptists. There are former missionaries from around the world. There are retired pastors and state workers. It is a humbling experience just to be there.

It was warm that night. The room in which I spoke was very warm. My wife was seated with a little lady from our church who had gone to live there. She could see the problem I was having with perspiration running from my head into my eyes.

My wife said to her, "It is really warm in here, isn't it?" The little lady replied, "Yes, it is just wonderful how warm they keep it for us older folks." By the time I finished my talk, I was damp from perspiration.

Just as we got to the door to leave, a cloudburst came. Rain came down in sheets. I told my wife to go to the covered entrance and I would get the car and meet her there. I was already damp and a little rain couldn't hurt.

Since my running days are over, I decided to take a shortcut across the lawn that separated the parking lot from the building. Just as I stepped on the lawn, the timer on the lawn watering system turned on. Water was now coming up as heavy as it was coming down. My shoes filled with water. My pockets filled with water. I did not have a dry thread on me.

I was grateful that I had felt so humbled to be there. If I had had any pride left in me, it would have been washed away before I got to my car.

# Hello, Mary Blaine

It was a lovely Sunday afternoon when my daughter, my son and I visited the old Presbyterian church just north of town. The old building was still open from the morning service. The custodian gave us a tour and a book of the church's history. The tombstones in the church cemetery date back to the 1700s. One of them is inscribed in English, French and Arabic.

We located this stone and then looked at many of the others there. One stone was inscribed: MARY BLAINE, CONSORT OF WILLIAM G. BLAINE. William was buried in the adjoining grave. My son asked the meaning of the word "consort." I said it must mean "mistress." I was later to learn that it was an old word for "wife."

I stepped on the grave to get a good look as I copied the word down. The grave suddenly collapsed. I sank down to my waist. I had just dropped in on Mary Blaine, unannounced. She wasn't much to

look at after 200 years.

My daughter ran for the car. My son fell to the ground in laughter. I had to pull myself from the grave without any help. My Sunday suit had mud on it from the waist down.

As we drove back to town, my son was rolling in laughter. I asked him if he really thought it was that funny.

"It will be when it is run in the newspaper," he said.

I asked him if it would be funny news to report that I had fallen in a grave.

"Oh, no," he said. "But when those reporters get through with it, it will read, 'Rev. Horace Sims Buried With Consort.'"

# Doughnuts

My exercise program is a little different from that of most of my friends. I begin every morning up and down, up and down, ten times. Then I exercise the other eyelid. After that, I put one foot on the floor, and if it is not too cold, I put the other foot out and get up. I then head for the shower with thoughts of doughnuts on my mind.

When I was in high school, I delivered a morning paper route. One Saturday morning, I met my Sunday school teacher pushing his car down the street. I asked him if he was having car trouble. He said he was just pushing the car down the street before he cranked it so he would not wake up his wife.

It seems she had put him on a diet. He said he had been lying in bed awake for several hours, watching doughnuts float around the ceiling. He was on his way to the doughnut shop for an early morning snack. I always liked that trait in my Sunday school teacher.

My love for doughnuts just seemed to come naturally. I always liked the smell of those yeast-raised, homemade doughnuts on the hearth at home. Mama would deep-fry them for our dessert. I can still smell them.

Well, it was following the evening session of the state convention that a group of us pastors went to a doughnut shop for a good bed-time snack. The doughnuts were still hot, and the coffee was fresh. We were having a great time before retiring for the night.

Then, a group of women came into the shop. One was on a diet. Why she came, I'll never know. She was dead set against doughnuts. She soon became obnoxious. It seems her doctor had told her dough-nuts were very fattening. He said they were coated in pure sugar and were bad for your health. She seemed to look right at me when she said that.

I said, "Ma'am, your doctor doesn't know what he's talking about. That's not sugar on those doughnuts. That's artificially-sweetened paraffin wax."

She said, "I know what my doctor said."

I replied, "I know from experience. Look at me, I eat two dough-nuts every night."

She gave me a thorough stare. I could tell from her look that I had not convinced her at all.

## Here Comes Santa Claus

Christmas is an exciting time of year. It's a time for great music and pageants. It's a time to be in church and listen to the great story of Jesus' birth.

Christmas has its secular side also. It's a time of parades and beau-tifully decorated trees. It's a time of gift-buying and of crowded stores and malls. And, whether in the spirit of the season or in person him-self, it's a time for Santa Claus.

Children have different responses to the old fellow. I like to sit and watch them as they are brought to see him. Some run to him, others run crying back to Mama.

I've been accused of being Santa Claus. As I left the mall one day, a little boy and his granddaddy were sitting in their truck. The little boy shook his dozing granddad and said, "There he is, Papa."

Papa asked him who he saw. The boy replied, "That's Santy Claus, that's him right there." I told the boy that I was not Santa, but that he could see him in the mall.

The next day, in a different store, a man said, "You're the man who plays Santa Claus at the mall."

"Do I look like Santa Claus?" I asked.

He replied, "I don't know if Santa has hair under that cap or not. And the beard is false."

I told my wife that these two false identifications did not make me Santa Claus. So, we went on to supper in one of our favorite restaurants. As we opened the door, a music box began to play, "Here Comes Santa Claus."

## Bursting Out All Over

My son and I have always enjoyed attending the annual meeting of the South Carolina Baptist Convention. We strolled into the big Carolina Coliseum on the campus of the University of South Carolina. We were met immediately by a man who asked if I still lived in Laurens.

"No, I now live in Greenwood," I said.

"How long have you lived there?" he asked.

"Oh, about 23 years," I replied.

"You never did live in Laurens, did you?" he asked.

"Not that I remember," I said.

We left this bewildered man staring at us and entered the main hall. As we started down the steps, one of the brass buttons popped off of my son's blazer. He thought we should return to the motel right then. I convinced him to leave his coat unbuttoned and no one would notice.

For lunch, we went to a small hot dog restaurant on the university campus. My son got a booth while I got the hot dogs. The booths were made for little college people. They were not made for fully-developed Baptist preachers. As I slid across the seat, my pants leg inseam ripped open from the crotch to the cuff.

I always keep the safety pins from the dry-cleaning tags in my pants waist. I slowly made my way across the restaurant to the restroom. It seemed that everybody in the place knew me. They all had to speak. They all smiled at the funny way I was walking.

Once back at the hotel, my wife asked what had happened to us. My son replied, "That thing broke out in the worst fight you have ever seen. Daddy and I were just lucky to get out with our clothes torn."

Come on down to the convention. You really can have a lot of fun.

## Orange Chair

I bought my son a student desk when he entered junior high school. I picked up a desk chair at the flea market. It was a swivel chair with chrome legs and a bright orange seat and back.

My wife didn't like it to start with. She said the color was tacky. I soon found it in the garage with a lot of other junk. I took it back to the flea market, but he would not take it back. He said he could not resell that color. That's not what he said when he sold it to me.

Well, my wife put it in a yard sale for $5. After the sale, the chair was back in the garage. At the next yard sale, it was priced for $3. Back to the garage it went. And at the last yard sale, the chair was offered as a bargain for $1.

This time, my wife refused to put it back in the garage. She sat the chair at the end of the driveway by the trash cart. She even placed a bag of trash in it so the trash collectors would be sure to see it.

I watched as the trash truck came. They emptied the cart and took the bag from the chair. They looked at the chair and drove off with-

out it.

We sat the chair beside the street, with a sign taped to it which read, "Free chair." This morning, I took the orange chair to the Salvation Army. They took my chair away.

That old chair reminds me of the sins we let get into our lives. And, try as best we can, we cannot get rid of them. That is, until we come to the Savior, who takes away all our sins and sets us free.

## Duet With a Bird

A young minister can find a lot of help from some of our retired ministers. These men have already done what the young ministers are facing for the first time.

I remember the first time I was asked to conduct a graveside service. I had never done this, so I called a retired minister friend for advice. I told him I had also been asked to sing at the graveside. He said he could not help me with the song. But he did give me some pointers for the service.

I followed his pointers, and that part of the service went fine. I had decided to sing just before the closing prayer.

The song had to be a cappella, since there was no way to get a musical instrument to the graveside. I had been asked to sing the beautiful hymn, "How Great Thou Art."

When I sang the words, and feel the gentle breeze, a cold wind blew through the tent. I could see the people shudder in the cold wind.

When I sang the words, and hear the bird sing gently in the trees, a little bird came out of a bush right at my shoulder and began to sing along with me. It was the first time I had ever sung with a bird.

A minister friend sitting with the family said that if anything else had happened, he was going to go to his car.

"You would have had to be right behind me," I replied.

## Wedding Mistakes

Preachers are called on to do a lot of tough jobs. One of those tough jobs for me is officiating at weddings. It is one of those times when no one wants anything to go wrong, especially the bride's mother.

There was the time the soloist was to be the signal for the groom and me to make our entrance. The organist played and played. The ushers and bridesmaids took their places. The bride and her father started down the aisle. The groom and I hurried to meet them at the altar. The soloist had forgotten to sing. People said they had never seen a wedding like that. I hadn't either.

And there was the wedding I sweated out. Just before time to take the groom out, my office phone rang. A lady said she had put a bomb in the altar flowers. I was sure it was a hoax and went on with the wedding. If there had been one popping sound, I would have been the first one out the door.

Well, then I was conducting a wedding in another church. The candles were high above us on the platform. The pipe organ was at full throttle. The vibration of the organ caused one of the candles to fall. It swished right by my ear and slid down my robe. I fully expected to burst into flames.

I had ragged one of my friends about one of his slips at a wedding. He told me that my day would come. Payday came at my own son's wedding. I said to his lovely bride, "You may now put the fing on his ringer."

Mama hasn't forgotten. My friend feels justified. My son has begun to speak to me again. His lovely bride just laughs.

## Stolen Robe

I suppose all churches have experienced some form of vandalism. We have had our share. Thieves have broken in and stolen cameras, a microphone, Cokes from the church kitchen and two pennies. The pennies were in two rice bowls on my desk.

The one big theft was that of my baptismal robe. My baptismal outfit was the gift of one of the couples in my church. I have always enjoyed using it.

Well, a city policeman came by my study one morning with my baptismal robe. He said the robe had been found in one of the streets of our community. Someone had told him that they thought it belonged to me. He said he was sure the thief was already in custody.

It was a cold, wintry night the night before. The thief had broken into the church seeking a warm place to spend the night. He sat on the pulpit platform and drank a bottle of cheap whiskey. He left the bottle behind.

Feeling the warmth of the bottled spirit, he suddenly felt called to preach. He found my baptismal robe in a closet and put it on. He then felt led to go into the community and preach to his friends.

Along the way, he gave up preaching as a bad idea. He discarded my robe in the street and fled. He was soon arrested by the police for public drunkenness.

He was brought to trial for theft and disorderly conduct. The police held my robe for evidence. At the trial, the judge asked if the robe had been identified. The officer stated that it had.

He said, "The robe belongs to the Rev. Horace Sims of Abney

Memorial Baptist Church."

"Is Rev. Sims' name in the robe?" asked the judge.

"No, sir," replied the officer.

The judge then asked how the robe had been identified. The officer held the robe up before the entire courtroom and said, "Your honor, you see the size of the robe, and I think you know Rev. Sims."

"I accept that as sufficient evidence," the judge said. With that, the thief got three years in jail.

I've always thought that this poor, cold, drunk thief got himself in trouble because he was not man enough to fill the robe.

# Ball-Ball

Have you ever thought about church without children? They are the spice that adds life to a church. It is a poor church that does not have children. They rustle the bulletin, cry, talk, laugh, and move back and forth on the pew. These are the noises of life.

My favorite time in the worship hour is the children's sermon. They come down the aisle with wide-open eyes. They are full of excitement and expectation. They will answer questions and enter right in the discussion.

After one children's sermon, I started back up on the platform. One little boy tugged at my coattail. I stepped back down on the floor and asked what he wanted. "Pray for my dog," he said.

"What's wrong with your dog?" I asked.

"He has ticks," he replied.

I told him we would pray for his dog.

"Right now," he demanded.

So, I prayed for a dog with ticks right then.

Our new neighbors had moved to town from one of the northern states. Their little girl was about a year old when they arrived. She was a little afraid of me. She would not let me hold her. However, she

made friends with my son immediately. He would walk around the yard with her in his arms.

He would rub the top of my head and say "ball-ball." It wasn't long before she was repeating his words. In fact, the whole family called me "Ball-Ball."

The family made a visit to church. They sat right in the middle. The music began. The choir took its place. The music director and I took our places on the platform. Just as the music stopped, a small voice was heard from the middle of the congregation. "It's Ball-Ball."

And so the title stuck.

## An Unscheduled Visit

"The pastor is coming to visit," Mama would say. She would then put us to work cleaning the house and the yards. The pastor ate Sunday lunch at our house once every year. He usually made a return visit to check on the spiritual condition of the family. There was always coffee and pound cake.

On one occasion, the pastor and one of the deacons made an unscheduled visit to our home. We were in the back yard, playing baseball with a ball of twine and a broom handle. My sister hit Daddy with the ball of twine. He began to chase her around the house with the broom handle in his hand. As they came to the front yard, there stood the pastor and the deacon on the front porch.

It took a lot of talking to convince Daddy that he could go to church again.

While in my first pastorate, I stopped by a home for an unscheduled visit. It was raining, so I went to the carport door to get out of the rain. I drew my fist back to knock on the door. Just as I came forward, the man of the house opened the door. I almost hit him on the end of the nose.

He jumped backward and said, "Good Lord, preacher, you scared the devil out of me." I felt a strong sense of satisfaction. My mission had been accomplished.

## Small Town Politics

Small town politics can be amusing. They can also pit family member against family member and church member against church member.

One of our town's personalities was always running for the office of governor. His speeches were exciting. He said, "My worthy opponent promises free textbooks for our school children. If I'm elected, I'll see that they get four and maybe five textbooks."

He also promised to get rid of detours. He pronounced them "daytours." He said, "When a man is on business, he don't have time to take a tour through the countryside."

You could always tell when it was election time. All of the politicians would show up at church. They would stand out front and welcome everybody as they arrived.

You knew who they were from all the posters nailed to the power poles.

Now, my dad had one of the longest memberships in my home church. His dad was one of the early deacons who signed the note with the bank to build the original building. Dad was baptized when he was nine years old. When Dad died, he had been a member of the church more than 70 years.

It was during one of these election times when our family was entering the church. As we approached the front door, one of the candidates for town mayor shook Daddy's hand and said, "We sure are glad to have you and your fine family visiting with us today."

Daddy thanked him as we went inside.

Once inside, Daddy said, "He's crazy if he thinks I'm going to vote for him. I've been here all my life."

## Good Clear Language

Children don't always understand adult figures of speech. They have a tendency to take things literally. They just don't understand what we mean.

I sent my son to clean his room. He played more than he cleaned. I said to him, "Come on, boy, shake a leg." My wife looked into his room and began to laugh. He was standing at the foot of his bed, shaking his left leg as hard as he could.

I came into the house, soaking wet from a sudden rain. I said, "Boy, it's raining cats and dogs out there." My daughter climbed up on the sofa and looked out the window. "I don't see any cats and dogs in our yard," she said.

When my son was young, he went to spend the weekend with some friends. Of course, he went to church with them. The preacher used some very colorful words to describe what he was talking about.

When he returned home, my son said the preacher had seen cars with gods on the back of them.

I asked him if he had seen any cars with gods on the back of them. He said no. He had ridden to church with someone else and they did not see any gods. I asked him if he had seen any cars towing motor boats. He said he had. I told him those were the gods the preacher had seen.

There is nothing like good clear language.

## Kegs and Barrels

My wife came to the door just as I was taking my latest treasure out of the trunk of the car.

"What is that?" she asked.

"A wooden nail keg," I replied.

"And what are you going to do with a wooden nail keg?"

"Every man needs a wooden nail keg."

When I came into the house, I told her the story of my first nail keg. My great uncle gave me a keg when I was nine years old. I thought it was the best gift I had ever gotten. I wouldn't let anybody play with my keg.

It finally came apart. I tied two of the staves to my feet and pretended to ski. Daddy nailed one of the hoops to the chinaberry tree for a basketball goal. I later sanded two of the staves and put confed-

erate soldier decals on them and hung them in my bedroom as plaques.

My wife said, "I hope you are not planning to do anything like that with this keg." I told her I was going to put some of my walking canes in it and sit it in the corner of the den.

"Wrong," she said.

I reminded her of our visit to Carl Sandburg's house in Flat Rock, North Carolina. There was a wooden nail keg full of walking canes sitting right by the grand piano in the living room. Without changing her expression, she looked me face to face and said, "You are no Carl Sandburg." So my nail keg is in the garage and my canes are in a ceramic churn.

Well, the other day my daughter met a pastor friend with a truck load of trash. In the truck was a large wooden barrel. She asked him what he was going to do with the barrel. "Take it to the dump," he replied. She told him she sure would love to have it. He took it to her house and sat it right at the end of the drive.

When her husband came home, he asked what she had that big wooden barrel for. "Every woman needs a wooden barrel," she said.

Now that's a girl after her daddy's own heart.

# Chapel Speaker

I was a young, inexperienced pastor at my first small church. Not many important invitations come to young, inexperienced pastors. However, I received what I thought to be a very challenging invitation. The invitation came from the chaplain at the Baptist Hospital. He wanted me to speak on the closed circuit, televised chapel program. The service could be seen on every television in the hospital.

The big day came. I made sure my only suit was well pressed and my shoes shined. My wife trimmed my hair so that I would look neat. I went to the study to put the finishing touches on my message. I had no doubt that this would be one of the most important messages I had ever delivered.

I left the study in time to drive to the hospital. Just as the study door closed and locked, I remembered my car keys were still lying on the desk. Our building was constructed of cement blocks. The doors and door frames were made of steel. I beat on the door. I ran into the door and almost dislocated a shoulder. The door would not give.

I decided to go outside and try one of the study windows. Just as I got outside, a cloudburst came. The church door had locked behind me. The study windows were also locked.

Panic began to set in. I knew that I was going to miss my big chance to do something important. In desperation, I took a small rock and pecked a hole in the window glass just behind the lock. With a small stick, I pushed the lock open. I climbed over the window sill and got my keys from the desk. As I passed the men's restroom, I saw myself in the mirror. My soaking wet suit was covered in white paint from the collar of my coat to the cuff of my pants.

I rushed home to change clothes. I put on whatever I had that was dry. Nothing matched. I looked like a clown. I made a mad dash for the hospital. I arrived at the chapel 15 seconds before the service was to begin. The chaplain asked, "Where have you been?"

I replied, "You really don't want to know."

With that, I stood before the television camera and delivered the most important seven-minute sermon in my young career.

## Locked In

Our church has been burglarized many times. We have tried many ways to prevent this. We installed solid wooden doors. We replaced glass with shatterproof Plexiglas. We covered all windows with storm windows. We installed outdoor lighting that comes on at dark. We finally placed the best deadbolt locks on all the doors.

At last, we seemed to be successful. We made our building secure. In fact, we may have made it too secure. One member thinks this may be true.

One of the deacons had an early afternoon tee time at the Star Fort Country Club. It seems he brought his golfing clothes with him. He went into the men's room after the service to change.

I walked down the hall and rapped on the men's room door. "Lights out," I yelled. When no one answered, I stuck my hand in the door and cut off the lights. I continued out the outside door and set the deadbolt.

The deacon groped in the darkness until he found the light switch. He rushed into the hall and yelled, "Wait on me." No one heard him. We had not only locked the crooks out; we had locked a deacon in.

He went through the building until he found one small door without a deadbolt. He escaped just in time to hit the ball.

## Bible Truth

How correct are the Bible stories you teach your children? I grew up wondering why Mama let us eat apples if they were so bad for Adam and Eve. I later found out that the Bible does not say they ate apples. The Bible states in Genesis 2:17 that they ate of "the tree of the knowledge of good and evil."

Now, what about Daniel and the lion's den? The lion's den is the habitat of the lion. He may or may not be home. The Bible states in Daniel 6:16 that he was thrown into a "den of lions." That's a big difference. In a "den of lions," the lions are at home, waiting for supper to be thrown in.

As a boy, I heard an old-time evangelist talk about the time God knocked Paul off his horse on the Damascus Road. However, Acts 9:4 states that "he fell to the earth." This was in reaction to the bright light that shone about him. There is a difference in falling and being knocked down.

When asked to name four apostles, most will say, "Matthew, Mark, Luke and John." These are the four gospels, but Mark was not an apostle. He was a fellow worker with the Apostle Peter.

I had the opportunity, with several other young preachers, to sit and talk with the great Methodist preacher Charles L. Allen. We were engaged in a lot of lighthearted talk. Dr. Allen looked at me and asked, "How many of each species of animals did Moses take on board the ark?" I said, "You are not going to catch me on that one. The Bible states in Genesis 6:19: 'Of all flesh, two of every sort.' The answer is two."

Hey, wait a minute. Did he say "Moses"?

# Junk Food

I sat by Mama's bed at the health care facility. We talked about all the food she used to eat. She's now at that point in her life where she will not eat.

I asked, "Did you ever eat possum?"

"Yes," she replied.

"How about poke salad?" I asked.

She always liked both of them together.

I asked her about rabbit, squirrel, turtle and frog legs.

"That's all good eating," she replied.

Then I asked, "Did you ever eat coon?"

"Did I ever eat what?" she asked.

"Coon," I said. "You know, when your brothers went coon hunting, did you eat any of the coon they brought back?"

"No, I never ate any junk like that," she said.

I wondered about all that other stuff if coon was junk.

Poke salad is the young leaves from the pokeberry plant. The big leaves and the berries are poison.

A possum looks like a big rat to me. I read once that when you had prepared the possum to be baked, you should slip it into your neighbor's oven because it stinks.

I have never eaten any of these delicacies. I eat beef, pork, fish and chicken. I'm not fond of rat-looking animals.

Well, the children in Sunday school were talking about their grandparents. They each took time to brag about what their grandparents owned. My son, not to be outdone, said, "My Nanny has two possums frozen in her freezer."

When he told Mama what he had said, she said, "Well, I'll never come back to your church again."

# Hungry Bum

The main job of the preacher is to proclaim the gospel. It is telling the old, old story of Jesus over and over again. The old, old story must be told as fresh as today's news.

There are many ways this can be done. It can be done through music, drama, dialogue and monologue. I was introduced to the effective use of dramatic monologue by the Rev. Earl Vaughan.

I have written several monologues on Bible characters for my own use. I usually do these in full costume. I was once asked to come to one of our local schools and read the Christmas story to the students before they left for the Christmas break. I asked the principal if I could do a costumed monologue instead. I dressed as one of the shepherds and told the story of Jesus' birth. After my program, the principal asked the students the name of the character who had spoken to them. Several Bible names were given. One little boy said, "It wasn't any of them, it was Preacher Sims."

One of my favorite monologues is one about Christmas on a mill village in 1930. It was written by C.M. Bissell of Saxon Mill in 1930. I dress the part of a mill hand of that period. I have presented this monologue many places.

One invitation for this monologue was to do it at the banquet the night before the Foreign Mission Board commissioning service at Clemson University. I was told I could change into my costume in the football locker room. I was then to wait in the hall to be introduced.

Now, this hall was the same one that the catering service had parked all of the food trays and cabinets in. A waiter came out to get a tray of food and saw me standing there in my costume. He thought I was a bum from the street. Another young man came out and placed himself between me and the carts. I asked him if he would get me a glass of tea. He said, "No, you are not even supposed to be in here."

I assured him I was a minister who was going to do a monologue. He replied, "Oh, yeah." I opened my old mill hand's lunch box and showed him my script and my name tag. He asked, "Do you want sweetened or unsweetened tea?"

I don't really guess I should have been surprised to find the football locker room locked when I went back to change into my dress clothes.

## I Like Ministerial Students

I like ministerial students. There is something exciting about students who have grasped great truths for the first time. Their enthusiasm is catching.

Ministerial students know the value of studying church history. They read Augustine, Luther, Calvin and Zwingli. They find inspiration as they meet these great men through their writings.

These students study Baptist history also. They know the importance of our history. Test your skills as you ask them about Keach, Bunyan, Gill, Fuller or Carey.

Ministerial students have the fire of evangelism in them. They know that Jesus Christ is the answer to the world's problems and they want to let the whole world know. They have not given up on lost souls being saved.

Ministerial students love to preach. They are usually good preachers. They still realize their sermons must be bathed in prayer. They may not be polished speakers, but they can be powerful in their messages.

Ministerial students pray. Their prayers are sincere and fervent. They have not gotten beyond dependence on prayer. They are not so self-assured that they feel they can go it alone.

So study and pray and preach, young man. Don't be hindered in your conquest for the Lord by us older fellows who have grown cynical and cold from battles fought and lost.

## Hot Tomatoes

Senior citizens are a fun group to be around. The majority of them are still excited about life.

Senior citizens are divided into three groups. The first group is the No-Go group. They are the ones who always stay at home. The second group is the Will-Go group. They will go if you come and get them. The third group is the Go-Go group. They are standing at the door, with their bags packed, waiting for the next bus.

I have spoken to many senior groups across the state. They love a good story and will give a hearty laugh. It is also a good place to get a good home-cooked meal.

I was invited to speak at a congregate meal site in Greenville. My mother and dad ate there each day. I think that probably had something to do with the invitation. My director of missions went with me.

We planned to visit another association meeting that evening.

Now, the people who eat at these sites are not supposed to bring any food with them. But they don't seem to know that. After the trays were passed out, the ladies got plates of biscuits, jars of jam and pickles.

One little lady had a jar of pickled tomatoes. She offered me one. Now, that is not one of my favorite things, but I was the guest, so I took one. I sliced the tomato in half and popped one half into my mouth.

I had never put anything that hot in my mouth before. My director of missions said I turned pale, and my eyes set. He thought I was having a stroke or something. I felt like I was on fire from my mouth to the bottom of my feet. I gulped down several cups of cold tea in an attempt to get relief.

The little lady asked, "Are those hot?"

"Hot is not the word," I replied.

"Well, I took the peppers out before I brought them," she said.

I think I shall be eternally grateful that she did not bring the peppers to that lunch.

## Christmas Tree Rodeo

Well, it's time to decorate the church for Christmas. The ladies always do a good job of getting the sanctuary ready for the season.

Red poinsettias are placed on the pulpit platform and in each window. They are also placed in the vestibule. The communion table is covered with the advent wreath. Different groups light the advent candles each week until all are lit.

A beautiful crismon tree stands just to the right of the platform. The ladies hand-made all of the crismons for the tree. It is always a live tree and fills the sanctuary with a sweet smell.

Our first tree was quite an experience. It was a big tree. It completely dwarfed the truck that brought it to the church. It took several men to bring it into the church. A stand had been constructed by the men to place the tree in. Everything was ready. It was time to stand the tree upright in the new stand.

It was so large that it needed to be counterbalanced from the top. A rope was secured to the top of the tree. Mary, a lady in the church, and I were given the task of pulling the rope to help the tree stand upright.

The tree slowly rose to a standing position. The men were guiding the bottom end of the trunk into the stand. At that moment, the tree bucked out of the stand and began to fall across the sanctuary. Mary and I were holding on to the top rope.

The tree fell across the sanctuary, almost hitting the lights. Mary and I held on for dear life. We rode the tree across the sanctuary like two rodeo riders. There are a lot of things I had rather do than ride a cedar tree bareback across a church sanctuary.

Each year since, I have been busy when it's time to raise the crismon tree in the church.

# I Like Preachers

I like preachers. I have always liked preachers. My boyhood pastor was my idol. I liked the way he preached. I liked his gestures while preaching. I liked him because he liked young people.

Preachers are different. They are under a call from God. They must always be ready to speak a word for the Lord. They must always be ready to pray. They are never off work. They are on call 24 hours a day.

Preachers are a lot like magicians. They must take the gospel story and weave it into a sermon that will reach young and old alike.

They can see a sermon rejected and trampled on, and yet build a new one for next Sunday.

Preachers who are really great are humble. They do what they do for the glory of God, not for themselves. They can see someone else get credit for what they have done and join the praise themselves.

Preachers have large emotional reserves. They cry with those who cry and laugh with those who laugh. They mourn with those who hurt and celebrate with those who rejoice. And they have to change from one emotion to the other with the snap of a finger.

Preachers appreciate hearing "That was a good sermon, preacher" from one of the deacons.

And they appreciate the little lady who says, "Thank you for your prayer, pastor."

And they are filled with joy when they feel the tug at their trousers leg and look down into the face of a smiling child who says, "Hey, p'eecher, I love you."

# Signs of the Times

Signs offer a lot of interesting reading. A sign at a car lot near my church reads, "Good, clean cars. We finance. No credit check. 24-

hour wrecker service." I believe if you buy one of these cars, you will need the wrecker service.

While visiting a hospital, I saw this sign: "Pediatric floor. No children allowed." I guess if a child once gets off this floor, he can't come back.

There was this sign on the gate to a motel swimming pool: "Pool open 24 hours a day. No swimming at any other time." I suppose this was for people who liked to swim after hours.

In 1982, a banner across the front of the Spartanburg Auditorium welcomed the South Carolina Baptist Convention. Below, another banner announced a coming attraction. The two banners read, "South Carolina Baptist Convention, Ain't Misbehaving."

A few years earlier, the marquee on the Greenville Auditorium was in the process of being changed from the wrestling matches to the convention. It read, "South Carolina Baptist Convention, Return Grudge Match."

Each year our convention has a theme banner. This year it is "Strengthening Churches for Kingdom Growth."

That's a lot better than a return grudge match.

# My Resolutions

A resolution is a course of action determined to be seen through to completion. If not seen through to the end, it is worthless. Most New Year's resolutions are worthless.

I have made some resolutions that I can see through to completion.

I resolve not to smoke, chew tobacco, or dip snuff. I never have and I don't plan to start now.

I resolve not to go on a diet. I certainly can keep that one.

I resolve not to eat rice pudding. I made that resolution in the second grade and have kept it ever since.

What good are these resolutions? There is no challenge in them. I don't do those things anyhow. It doesn't take any determination to keep these resolutions.

The Apostle Paul offered us a four-part resolution in Hebrews 10:19-25. It is written in perfect parliamentary style. He offers three "whereas" statements and then the four-part resolution. He resolves to draw near to God, to hold fast to the hope we profess, to encourage one another to love and good deeds, and not to fail to meet together.

Each of these will take a lot of determination, but the rewards for doing so will be tremendous.

## The Way I Am

"What makes you the way you are?" someone asked me the other day. "You seem to be able to laugh with ease," he said.

"Well, I grew up so poor you either laughed or cried," I replied.

Since laughter is easier than crying, I chose to laugh. I guess I also learned to laugh in the school of hard knocks.

I walked about three miles to grammar school each day. One day, a friend's dad gave me a ride in his pickup truck. As we rounded a curve, the door flew open and I fell out. I rolled down the side of the road, hitting my head on several rocks. I got back into the truck, laughing so my friend would not see me crying.

Well, walking home from high school, I stumbled over a rock and fell head first into a rock wall that surrounded a neighbor's front yard. I knocked a hole in my head.

Now, my dad was a great inventor. He made most of our toys. We had things that could not be bought in the store. Somewhere Dad came across a large spring. He tied one end of it to a limb on the chinaberry tree. He hung another piece of rope from the other end of the spring. He tied it around a broomstick at about two feet from the ground. You could stand on the broomstick, hold onto the rope, and

bounce up and down.

I was taking a good ride on this contraption when the rope around the tree limb broke. The spring hit me on top of my head. I woke up in my uncle's Model A on the way to the doctor and his needle. My crying soon gave way to laughter.

Proverbs 17:22 reads, "A merry heart does good like a medicine." It may be that a merry heart can even make an old sorehead laugh.

# The Glowing Crucifix

There is something about the darkness that is both exciting and foreboding. I like to sit by the ocean and watch the sun set and the moon rise. The moon shining over the ocean is a beautiful sight.

But I don't like to be by the ocean on a real dark night. There is a feeling of danger there without the moon and the stars. The pounding of the waves is an uneasy sound in the dark. I guess I just like to be able to see in the dark.

When I was a boy, I spent a lot of time at my aunt's home in the country. They did not have street lights like we did in the city. It was really dark at night there when the moon did not shine.

One night, my cousin asked me to spend the night at her house. I wasn't used to having a bedroom all to myself. My brothers and I shared a bedroom at home.

After the lights were turned out, I saw a figure glowing in the dark. Trying hard to breathe, I found the light switch and turned on the light. There was nothing there. I repeated this several times. I finally realized the glow was coming from a crucifix on the wall. I kept my eye on it the rest of the night.

As the years have gone by, I have thought a lot about the message of that glowing crucifix. It lets me know that no matter how dark the journey of life may be, Jesus is always there to light the way.

# A Stopping Place

How long should a sermon be? I suppose that would have to be answered by the preacher and the listener.

The preacher wants to be sure he has said it all. The listener says, "You have said enough."

Those who teach preaching among Southern Baptists have suggested that a sermon be made of three points. A poem could be added to the end for special effect.

One of the best British preachers always used seven points. He usually quoted a couple of poems or hymns also. His sermons were expositional.

During one of the interim periods at our church, the preacher had been preaching for about 45 minutes.

One of the ladies said, "That was a long sermon today, preacher."

He replied, "I couldn't find a stopping place."

"You didn't ask me. I could have shown you at least three good places," she said.

One Sunday, I guess I had passed a good stopping place. I gave an emphasis to the sermon by asking, "Are you ready to go?" I meant, are you ready to stand before God.

One little fellow stood up on the pew and said very plainly, "I'm ready to go home!"

I thought that was a very good idea. So we stood, had prayer and went home. We had found a stopping place for my sermon.

## My Nativity Set

It was a cold and windy day as we drove the winding road from Jerusalem to Bethlehem. A light snow was falling as we arrived in the little village.

We quickly walked across the courtyard to the Church of the Nativity. We entered the church by crawling through a very small door. Our guide led us down a staircase to a cave below the church. Here, in this grotto, we were told, was the birthplace of Jesus. The church had been built over the site some centuries later.

God had chosen to enter human history in this little village of common people. It was a village of simple shepherds. God came to a people who lived with faith in the promise of a coming Messiah. God always comes to those who live by simple faith.

As we left Bethlehem, we stopped at an olivewood shop. The craftsmen here made gifts out of the wood of the ancient olive trees. I purchased a beautiful nativity set made completely out of olivewood. The shopkeeper put it in a large, purple box and tied it with twine.

He asked me what I was going to do with the nativity set when I got home. I told him I would use it as part of my Christmas decorations. "Why only at Christmas?" he asked. "Does it not mean anything the rest of the year?"

I took my nativity set back to my hotel in Jerusalem. I had been told that it would fold to fit in my suitcase. But the wood was glued together and could not be folded.

The only way to get my nativity set home was to carry it in the big, purple box tied with twine. I could not check the box as luggage. The box would not fit in the overhead luggage rack on the plane.

So, I flew from Tel-Aviv to Athens, Greece, with the purple box in my lap. I flew from Athens to New York to Atlanta to Greenville-Spartanburg with the purple box in my lap.

All the way home, I thought of the shopkeeper's question: "Why only at Christmas?" God's gift of salvation is a life-changing gift for all of eternity.

Have a very meaningful Christmas as you celebrate the unspeakable gift that God has given you.

## In the Name of Progress

The definition of the word "progress" is "to develop to a higher, better, or more advanced stage." Sometimes you wonder if everything that is called progress really fits this description.

I remember when a church that had a piano and an organ was a progressive church. It took someone with a lot of talent to play these instruments. Now, in the name of progress, we play tapes for our music.

I remember when my pastor preached that the Bible was literally true. He preached that hell was a real place of eternal punishment and that heaven was the home of the redeemed.

Now, in the name of theological progress, we are told some of the Bible is true, and some of the Bible is myth and legend. One progressive preacher said hell was simply the loss of self-esteem.

When I was a boy, Mama would wash the clothes in a tin tub on the wash bench in the back yard. After she finished with the clothes, we boys would strip off and take a bath right out there in the yard. We later got an indoor tub where we could take our baths in private.

Now, my neighbor has put his tub out on his deck. He gets in it right there before the whole community, and, in the name of progress, he calls it a spa.

## Just Pondering

To ponder means "to weigh mentally." It also means "to meditate on" or "to consider carefully." Some things take a lot of pondering. You should practice that ancient art from time to time.

In the past few weeks, I have had time to ponder some of the issues of life. These may not have been great issues, but I pondered them anyhow.

I pondered why my hair grows thicker on the left side of my head than on the right. My hairstylist brought this to my attention. I don't think it really means I am a half-wit.

I pondered why my right foot is larger than my left. My left shoe slips on while the right one requires a shoe horn. I guess the large right foot offsets the weight of the thicker hair on the left side of my head.

I like to ponder nature also. Why doesn't the quack of a duck have an echo? A duck can stand on the mountain all day quacking, but never an echo. And ponder this: Would thunder sound the same if there were no one to hear it?

A little theological pondering is needed also. When Peter saw the sheet let down from heaven, was it full, queen or king-size? Was it flat, or fitted?

I seem to be getting a headache from all of this pondering. It could be that the college advertisement is right: "A mind is a terrible thing to waste."

## Getting Things Right

Getting things right is important. After all these years, I still have to rely on the Sunday bulletin to get the order of worship right. It seems that I always get something out of place or just forget something.

A music minister friend of mine had some of this kind of trouble. Their morning service was broadcast live over radio. Now, there is no room for mistakes on a live broadcast.

The choir came out for the call to worship. The pianist began to play a hymn while the organist began to play a different hymn. The choir was singing yet a third hymn. Much to my friend's embarrassment, he stopped the music and got everybody on the same song. They finally got it right.

I had been inviting a friend to church for some time. I never really expected him to come. He said, "I'm going to show up some Sunday and surprise you."

Well, one Sunday I was singing a solo when my friend came into the vestibule, smiled and waved at me. I forgot the words to the song I was singing. I couldn't even hear the piano.

Years later, I noticed in the newspaper that my friend had died.

The obituary said he was a member of a Baptist church. It reported that he was the teacher of the men's Bible class. I had messed up the song, but ... I guess I got it right after all.

## Hospital Thrill Ride

I don't like thrill rides at carnivals or amusement parks. They seem to send my stomach spinning in a disturbing way.

You can get a thrill ride outside the amusement parks. They can take place in what may seem like an ordinary daily activity.

I was being moved from test room to test room on a flat cart. I was lying flat on my back, covered with a white sheet. I'm sure that I looked like a Sherman tank coming down the crowded hallway.

Two young men were in charge of my cart. We left the second floor by elevator to go to the fifth floor. When the elevator opened,

one of the young men said, "What are we doing in the basement?"

The other young man said, "Sorry about that, sir."

"That's all right," I said. "I would not have seen the basement any other way."

They returned me to the fifth floor. When we rolled off the elevator this time, we rammed a cart parked in front of the nurses station.

"How long have you boys had your drivers' licenses?" I inquired.

"Are you a highway patrolman?" one of them asked.

"No, I'm a Baptist preacher," I replied.

"That's just as bad," he said.

With that, they delivered me to my room and helped me get into my bed.

"We hope everything goes well with you," one of them said as they left the room.

"Take care of the cart!" I exclaimed.

# Hit It

It was a clear, hot day. We planned a trip to the Baptist Book Store in Greenville. We ate lunch at a fast-food restaurant before we left. We really did that to keep the children from saying "I'm hungry" all the way there.

As we left the restaurant, I waited for a chance to get into the traffic. When the break came, my son, who had just gotten his driver's license, leaned over the seat and said, "Hit it." Just to let him know I wasn't too old to know what that meant, I stepped down hard on the accelerator.

The car jumped and then backfired. It began to skip and knock. Black smoke boiled from the exhaust pipe. I tried to get it to settle down, but it got worse. We would have to have a mechanic to check it out.

Our mechanic was about four miles away. We knocked, skipped

and smoked all the way there. Just before we got there, the tail pipe and muffler came apart and began dragging the road.

The mechanic asked what had happened. "I hit it," I said with my head down.

"I believe you knocked it out," he replied. The car would not be ready until the next day. The trip to the Baptist Book Store was off.

Since we lived five blocks away, we decided to walk home. It was at least 100 degrees. Several church members passed by and honked. They thought we were walking for our health.

One lady stopped to offer us a ride. She had a very small car. We could not all fit into it. I told my wife and children to go home and come back and get me. My son came back to pick me up in his old Jeep. I crawled into it and he started off with a jerk.

"That's what I meant when I said, 'Hit it'," he said. I took one good look at him and thought to myself, if he says "hit it" one more time, I'm going to hit something—but it's not going to be the car.

## Passing Through the Doughnut Hole

The last few weeks have been exhausting for me.

I have been x-rayed from head to foot. I have become a fixture in the scan department.

A CAT scan is a big machine that looks like a giant, sugar-coated Krispy Kreme doughnut. Your body lies on a small, steel table while it passes back and forth through the middle of the doughnut.

Now, I had at least a foot overhang on each side of that little table. My arms had to be held in an unnatural position to keep from having

them jerked out of their sockets.

After spending hours in this contraption, I thought of a way to make it more bearable. It should be labeled in giant, green letters which read, "Fresh-baked doughnuts."

Can't you imagine the joy of passing back and forth through a giant, jelly-filled doughnut?

While I was lying on this table, the room filled with medical personnel. They began to attach different pieces of equipment to me.

It seemed I was going into surgery right there on the CAT scan table.

A doctor walked up with an eight-inch-long needle in his hand and asked, "Have I explained to you how I do a biopsy?"

I took a good look at the needle and just don't remember a lot after that.

## My Beliefs

We live in a day when we are all expected to have a creed or a confession of faith.

We use these creeds to judge our fellowship with each other.

So, let me tell you some things I believe.

I believe that we must love everybody. The Bible says, "For God so loved the world." This is an all-inclusive love. No one can be left out.

I believe that we must have compassion on everybody. The Bible says when Jesus saw the multitude, he was moved with compassion on them. The church that puts any program ahead of compassion is a failure.

I believe we must meet the physical, as well as the spiritual, needs of the world. Jesus said when we feed the hungry, clothe the naked, give water to the thirsty, visit the sick and those in prison, we have done it unto him.

I believe we must preach the gospel of salvation to all the world. Jesus said we were to go into all the world. We are to win, teach and baptize.

I believe in prayer. Paul said we ought to pray all the time. The only real Christian is one who believes in prayer and practices it.

And I believe we ought to laugh. The Bible says the one who sits in the heavens shall laugh.

So, judge me by what I believe, if you wish.

I believe our faith is seen in more than our words.

## Just Talking ... Forever and a Day

However you say it—tempus fugit, tide and time wait for no man, time's a wastin'—they all mean the same thing: Time flies.

We are at the changing of the year. We are almost at the changing of a century. Ready or not, here it comes. The year 1998 is gone and, with it, all its hopes and dreams.

It has been said, "We grow too soon old and too slow smart." How did I get here so fast? It seems like only yesterday I was a barefoot boy in City View. And now I am almost three-score years old with a wife, two married children, and three precious grandchildren.

Once along this journey, due to a series of near-fatal heart attacks, I arrived at the gate to eternal life, but the good Lord sent me back. Now, having been diagnosed with inoperable kidney cancer which has spread to the lungs, I am on that journey toward the gate again.

The big question is, "Would I have done anything differently?"

The answer is yes. I would have prayed more. I would have spent more time with my children. I would have walked in the fields with my Lord and talked as old friends. I might have even gone fishing and maybe tried hunting.

God has been good to me. He gave me a wonderful, supportive

family. He let me spend 28 years already at the sweetest church in South Carolina. He even allowed me to meet and know Baptist people all across this state and beyond.

Do I have one wish left? I would love to sit in a quiet corner with my loving wife, sipping coffee and just talking … forever and a day.

# SECTION
## TWO

# Other
# Writings

## View From a Chinaberry Tree

You either love a chinaberry tree, or you hate it. It may be possible to do both. When you smell its sweet blossoms in the spring, you'll love it. When you sit under its cool shade on a hot day, you'll love it. When you have to rake up all those slimy berries in the fall, you'll hate it. If you have several chinaberry trees around your house, you may even lose your taste for English peas because those chinaberries look just like them.

Now, on the other hand, chinaberry trees are good for boys. They have low-spreading branches and are very easy to climb. In fact, several boys can sit in one tree at the same time. It is a good place for boys to have their very important conversations in. No doubt, many great decisions have been made in a chinaberry tree. You can sit in a chinaberry tree for most of the day. If you climb high enough, you can hide among the leaves and watch the world go by.

We had three chinaberry trees at our house. We had two in the front yard and one in the back yard. I think this was so that each one of us had his own tree. When you played cowboys and Indians, or cops and robbers, you needed your own hideout. A chinaberry tree was good for that.

Chinaberry trees were also very good for another reason. The berries made excellent ammunition for pea shooters. We would leave for school with a piece of bamboo cane in one pocket and a handful

of chinaberries in the other. A well-placed shot with a chinaberry could raise quite a welt.

A chinaberry tree could also be dangerous. On one occasion, my brother tried to make a Tarzan-like leap from his tree. He got his head caught between the forks of two limbs and hung himself. I wasn't tall enough to get him loose, so I ran to get Daddy. He lifted him up and freed him from certain death in a chinaberry tree.

I kind of miss the old chinaberry trees, but I can eat English peas again.

## Mama's Banking System

A person has to be pretty sharp just to bank his money these days. With IRAs, money market certificates, simple interest accounts, all-star accounts, instant cash accounts, installment loans, and joint checking accounts, banking gets to be somewhat confusing. I have enough trouble just balancing my checking account.

My mother never had these problems. When I was a boy, we never went to the bank. Mama had her own banking system.

Her bank was an oblong, tin cookie can with handles that folded across the top. This can contained an assortment of smaller ones. These were baking powder cans and Band-Aid cans. Some were even little banks themselves.

Each of these cans was for a different bill. Mama had worked out a budget that called for so much money to be put in each can each week.

One can was for insurance and taxes. Another was for lights and water. There was a can for groceries and one for clothes and doctors. One can was for the house payment, which was twenty-three dollars a month.

Now, sometimes a bill was higher than expected. She would then have to borrow from one of the other cans to meet the increase. When she did this, she would put the amount borrowed on a little slip of paper and place it in that can. The next week, the borrowed amount would have to be replaced.

Mama kept her bank under her bed. We all knew where it was, but none of us would ever get it out from under the bed unless Mama told us to do so. The cans were never locked up. They didn't need to be. We all knew that that money was our livelihood and none of it ever took missing.

When any of us children wanted a penny or maybe a nickel, we would go and ask Mama. She would say, "Go and get the can and let me see what I can do." I crawled under that bed many times to get the can out for a penny. That's when you could get two pieces of bubble gum for a penny. In the worst of times, Mama could always find a little money in her bank.

I can still see Mama and Dad at the big round table in the dining room, figuring out their bills. There on the table in front of them would be the cans and Dad's pay envelope. We never had much money, but we never went without the things we needed. Between Dad's pay and Mama's banking system, there always seemed to be enough to meet the need.

Recently, while rambling through an old cabinet at my home place, I found Mama's old banking system. My folks finally gave in and started using a commercial bank when they began to draw their Social Security checks.

I found the oblong, tin cookie can with three of the smaller tin cans that Mama had used for so many years. Two of the smaller cans were little banks. They were advertising cans for A&P Bokar and Eight O'Clock Coffee. Both of these cans must be about 50 years old.

My initials were scratched on one of these cans. When I became old enough to carry a paper route, Mama helped me with my banking. My two brothers' initials were also scratched on those cans. As they grew older, they took over the paper route and let Mama keep their money in her bank.

The third little can that was still in the bank was a Calumet Baking Powder can. It was so worn that most of the paint on the can was gone. On the top of this can was scratched a large "T." That "T" meant "turkey."

Thanksgiving Day was a big event at our home. Family would come from near and far to eat with us. We all still go home for Thanksgiving Day. We never had a Thanksgiving Day without a big turkey. Mama had put money in that Calumet can all year so that we could have our turkey.

Well, I've been sitting here looking at those cans and thinking about all that was accomplished by using them. I've even been wondering if they would work as well for me as they did for Mama.

Who knows? I may soon give them a try.

## Granny Smoked a Pipe

Long before the days of ERA, my granny smoked a pipe. In fact, her hobby was smoking the many pipes she received as gifts.

One of her pipes was a miniature replica of a commode, complete with seat and lid. The sender of this gift also included some twists of tobacco right from the curing shed on the farm. We all watched as Granny lit up the commode pipe for the first time. When the tobacco was burning, she closed the lid on the seat. She was really hacked when the fire burned a hole right through the lid of her pipe.

The favorite gathering place for our family was Granny's bedroom. The first radio I remember was in that bedroom. We gathered there to hear President Roosevelt give his fireside chats to the nation. I hardly knew what a president was, but I could see by the expressions on the adults' faces that he was an important man. I remember the night we heard over Granny's radio that President Roosevelt was dead. All those who had gathered there wept. I did, too. It just seemed the right thing to do.

We were sitting in Granny's bedroom when we heard the news of the end of the war. The next day, all the church bells in town rang out the good news. While we were celebrating, I saw Aunt Eade, who lived next door to Granny, standing at her back door, weeping. Her son had been killed in the war and would not be coming home. I began to believe that there must be something very bad about war.

Granny's bedroom was a favorite place for us boys. She always had a snack hidden somewhere. Granny believed in eating, a trait I seem to have inherited. She would make a sandwich and wrap it in wax paper. When night came, she would put the sandwich on the table by her bed. If she woke up hungry, she wouldn't have to go out to the kitchen to get something to eat. That always seemed like a good idea to me.

Early one morning, one of our aunts came to tell us that Granny was very sick. She said we should come to Granny's bedroom as soon as we could.

We all stood silently around the walls of our favorite gathering place. Granny was lying on her bed, staring at the ceiling. As we watched, she closed her eyes and slowly went to sleep forever. I walked back down the street to our house, heartbroken.

I doubt that I have been back in Granny's house more than twice since she died. I was 10 years old then, and it seems like such a long time ago. But I am grateful for the memories that linger—the big radio, the sandwich by the bed at night—and especially for the memory of my granny who smoked a pipe.

## Going for the Christmas Tree

I grew up in the city. We did not own an automobile. Daddy never knew how to drive, and we did not have a car until I learned to drive. We lived on the trolley line. Two trolley routes stopped right in front of our house—Belt South and Belt North. With a token and a transfer, you could ride all over town.

Each year at Christmas, we would make our annual trip to the country to get our Christmas tree. The trip was quite an adventure in itself. Mama would pack all our overnight clothes in an old sample case that Daddy had gotten at the plant where he worked. Then, early on a Saturday morning, we would ride the electric trolley to West Greenville. There we could catch the Welborn Bus Line to the country. It was a commuter line between Greenville and the towns in Pickens County.

Our trip took us through the little towns of Easley, Norris, Liberty, and to Central, where we got off the bus. Uncle Cephas Newton would be waiting for us. We got in his car for the rest of the trip to near the town of Six Mile.

On Saturday afternoon, Uncle Cephas would take us out to the woods to find a Christmas tree. We would look and look until we found just the right tree. Most times Daddy would climb up in a big cedar tree and cut just the top out for our Christmas tree. Then we headed back to the house, where Aunt Lucy would have a feast waiting.

The kitchen in Aunt Lucy's house was unusual. On one side it was a modern kitchen. On the other, it had a large fireplace in which she could cook over the open fire. It had a pot hook on either side for hanging pots of beans and turnip greens. She would cook biscuits and cornbread in Dutch ovens, which sat in the coals that had been pulled out onto the hearth. Food never tasted any better than when cooked over an open fire.

After breakfast on Sunday morning, we would all go to church with Aunt Lucy and Uncle Cephas. They went to the Mt. Olivet Wesleyan Church. It was something different for us six Baptists. After another feast for Sunday dinner, Uncle Cephas would load us and our Christmas tree in his car and take us back home to Greenville.

That was the beginning of our Christmas. The next days were filled with cleaning and decorating the house and helping bake the cakes and pies and candy for the big day, which was just around the corner.

## Homemade Fun

As I watched my son play with his new AK Centerfire Motorized Water Sub-Machine Gun, which shoots up to 30 feet, I thought about the way we entertained ourselves when we were young.

Most of our toys were homemade. We played cowboys and Indians with broomstick guns. Our bows and arrows were made from

young saplings and reeds. The coal bin was the jail, and chinaberry trees were our hideouts. You could always tell when somebody had been locked up in the jail.

We kept Daddy busy just making us something to play with. He made us a scooter from a pair of old roller-skate wheels. He put two of the wheels on the front and back ends of a piece of board and attached a handle and away we would go. I tried my hand at making one of those, but it didn't work as well as his did.

He also made us a pair of "tom-walkers" (stilts) from two-by-fours. I don't know why we called them tom-walkers, but we did. Once you learned how to stay up on them, they were really fun.

We also made walkers from empty oil cans that we got at the Esso station next door. We would punch holes in the side of the can and run pieces of cord through the holes to use for handles. The object was to pull on the cords so that the cans would stay against your feet and you could walk on them without falling off. My children had plastic versions of these that were called Romper-Stompers.

Some of Daddy's inventions did not work out as he had planned. He made us a kite out of newspaper and reeds. He doubled the newspaper so that the kite would not tear. The kite became airborne rapidly. The wind was very strong that day. The kite was even stronger. The string burned Daddy's hand so bad he had to turn it loose. We never saw our kite again.

Yes, I still remember the homemade slingshots, the wooden block cars and trucks, the spinning propellers made from fruit-jar lids, the bamboo whistles, the match stick darts, and I guess a hundred other things. They didn't cost much money, but they sure were fun.

## Mama's New Cook Stove

While browsing through a junk shop recently, I found a fuel reservoir for a kerosene cook stove. It was a one-gallon glass jar with a metal band around it, to which was fixed a wire handle. A valve of sorts was screwed to the opening at the neck of the jar. The jar would be inverted into the tank on the stove, and this valve would release the kerosene as needed. After a little bit of bargaining, I took the old jar home with me. It reminded me of one of my chores as a boy.

Our first cook stove was a kerosene stove. It had three burners and an oven. The burners were heated by the kerosene oil that came from the glass reservoir. My job was to make sure there was oil in the stove when Mama got ready to cook. I would take the jar to the little Esso station next door. Kerosene was kept in a red metal tank in the grease rack. The oil was pumped out into my little glass jar by means of a hand pump. A gallon of kerosene cost about 20 cents back then.

A few years after electric cook stoves became popular, Mama decided to get her one. Her first range was a small one known as an apartment-size range. The house had to have a special-size electric wire installed for Mama's new range.

The day finally came when Mama tried out her new cook stove. She turned the burner on, and we all stood waiting to see what would happen. The burner coils remained black. We continued to wait. Nothing seemed to happen. We were all beginning to feel let down by Mama's new stove. How could you cook on something that just sat there? I could just imagine life without fatback, biscuits, grits, and gravy.

Out of curiosity, Mama placed her hand on the black burner rings to see if they were getting warm. The sizzle and scream let all of us know that the new electric cook stove was working. Mama had a perfect set of burner rings burned into the palm of her hand for the next few weeks.

That was the first cooking that Mama did on her new electric cook stove.

## My Aunt Was a Real Princess

My aunt was a real live princess. Her name was Princess Nina Eristova Shervashidze. She was born in St. Petersburg in Russia. The daughter of Prince Eristoff Shervashidze, she grew up during the reign of Nicholas II.

Her father was an officer in the Czarist army. She knew the pomp and excitement of the Czar's palace. It was a way of life that she had been born into.

But things began to change in Russia. There was unrest among the working people of the country. Names like Trotsky and Lenin began to be heard. The beginning of a revolution could be felt in St. Petersburg and in Moscow and Petrograd. The discontent grew until a full revolution swept the country.

In March of 1917, Czar Nicholas I abdicated his throne. He and his family were exiled to Yekaterinburg in Siberia. Some of his official staff accompanied him there. Aunt Nina and her family were among those who went with the Czar.

Some of the Bolsheviks were not satisfied that the Czar had been allowed to go into exile. So they followed him to Yekaterinburg. There, in the basement of one of the buildings, they murdered the Czar and most of his family. Aunt Nina's father was one of those who died.

One of the most famous stories to be told about this event has to do with the escape of the Czar's daughter, Anastasia. Many women have claimed to be the real Anastasia. But there were others who also escaped. Among those were Aunt Nina and her mother.

They were able to take refuge in Georgia in the Balkans. Finally, in 1920, they were able to escape from Russia. Aunt Nina used her talent as a ballerina to earn money to help her and her mother make their way across Europe and eventually to the United States.

Aunt Nina was educated in schools in Massachusetts and Pennsylvania. After she had completed her education, she and her mother went to live with some Russian friends in Mexico. They were friends who had also escaped the Bolshevik revolution.

Mexico, however, did not prove to be safe for Russian exiles. Following the death of Lenin, Stalin proclaimed himself leader of Russia. He and Leon Trotsky could not agree on policies. So, Trotsky fled to Mexico. There, some time later, he was assassinated by a Russian agent.

Aunt Nina and her mother, not satisfied with conditions in Mexico, came back to the United States. Upon her return, she began to work for the State Department. She was proficient in five languages. This made her a valuable during World War II.

Now, the story of how this beautiful Russian princess became my aunt begins here. My mother's brother had earned the rank of Brigadier General in the United States Army. He was Adjutant General to General Douglas MacArthur. Later, he would become Adjutant General to General Dwight Eisenhower, and finally Assistant Chief of Staff of the Army under General George Marshall.

One of General MacArthur's biographers described my uncle, Brigadier General Thomas Jefferson Davis, as being as southern as his name. Well, this southern-born and southern-bred general met this Russian-born and Russian-bred princess, and they fell in love. It was a real-to-life fairy tale.

Uncle Tom met Aunt Nina while she was performing as a ballerina. He was awestruck with the beauty of this Russian princess. You might say that she danced her way right into his heart. They were married in a double ceremony with General MacArthur and Jean Faircloth on board a ship in the harbor of Shanghai, China, on May 25, 1937.

I remember every visit that they made to our home. In those days, the adults ate first and the children waited until last. When the preacher came for dinner, we sat on the back door steps until our time came. But when Uncle Tom and Aunt Nina came, we asked to be allowed to sit on the floor against the dining room wall so we could hear the conversation.

There we sat spellbound as this handsome general in his ribbon-bedecked uniform and his Russian princess wife ate and talked with Mom and Dad. Listening was enough. We never dared to enter into the conversation.

Once I did venture to enter into the adult conversation. The General looked at me very sternly and said, "Young man, I was speaking to your mother." That scared me so bad that I slipped out to my bedroom and hid under the bed.

In a little while, I heard footsteps coming into my room. Looking out from under the bed, I saw two black military shoes. Then Uncle Tom knelt down on one knee and looked at me under the bed.

"My, my, what a big man," he said. Then, in a strong military voice, he commanded me, "Come out from under that bed." I came out so fast that I almost took all the hair off the top of my head on the bed rails.

The General laughed a big laugh, put his arm around my shoulder and walked me to the store to get a big bag of candy. He topped the day off by taking us to ride in his pretty, new Lincoln Zephyr.

After his retirement from the Army, Uncle Tom and Aunt Nina operated a pheasant farm near Central, South Carolina. They were the object of many newspaper articles. They were very active campaigners for General Eisenhower when he ran for the office of President. They were his personal guests at his inauguration.

They later moved to San Antonio, Texas. There Uncle Tom died at the age of 81. Aunt Nina, heartbroken and grief-stricken, died shortly thereafter.

Of all my many mementos, my favorite one is a picture of Uncle Tom, Aunt Nina and me. I stood almost up to their waists, and if you look real close, you might see a little look of pride. For, after all, how many of my friends had a real live princess for an aunt?

## Southern Baptist Convention Tales

A funny thing happened at the convention. It may sound like an overused cliché, but it is true. Some of my most interesting experiences have taken place while attending the Southern Baptist Convention.

Being from the South, I am an old grits eater from way back. So I was certainly surprised to find that the restaurants in Dallas didn't serve grits. I left my hotel at the Market Area and went downtown early every morning to get ahead of the crowd. But I couldn't find a restaurant that served grits.

As we were flying back from the convention, a friend asked me how I liked Texas. "Fine," I said, "except for the fact that they do not serve grits."

"Where did you eat breakfast?" she asked.

"Downtown," I replied.

"You should have eaten at the hotel," she said. "They ordered grits just for us South Carolinians."

I felt a little foolish, being an old grits eater staying at a hotel full of grits and not even knowing it.

Another unforgettable experience happened in a well-known Mexican restaurant in Dallas. We were all wearing our convention badges with our names, towns and states. Our waiter was a young man with a dark complexion, black hair, and a black mustache.

As he handed us our menus, he asked if we were all from South Carolina, and we told him that we were. I then asked him if he had ever been to South Carolina. He answered with a Mexican accent and said, "Yes, many times, señor." I asked him if he had been to Greenwood. He said, "I know it well, señor."

My friends asked him if he had been to their hometowns of Clinton, Abbeville and Laurens—all towns in a 50-mile radius in South Carolina. "I know them well," he answered. I then asked him why he had been to these small towns in our state. "Meeny relatives," he said. When I said that I had never seen any Mexicans in Greenwood, our waiter said, "I was born and raised in Newberry, South Carolina." Newberry is only 30 miles from Greenwood. "I dress and talk dees way to keep the job," he said. It turned out that the waiter's father was a deacon in one of my friend's churches.

Getting around in the large convention cities can be a challenge to some of us from smaller towns. We had made good time driving to New Orleans. As we crossed the Lake Pontchartrain Bridge, we were playing a Dixieland jazz tape on the tape player. I drove right into New Orleans, just like I knew what I was doing. We spotted the Super Dome right off. That was the first sighting, but before we could get off the interstate, we had passed the Super Dome several times, coming and going. When we finally got across the Mississippi to our hotel, a friend from South Carolina pulled up right behind me.

"Boy, was I wrong," he said.

"What do you mean?" I asked.

"I thought you knew where you were going," he replied.

I have always liked to take part of Monday to sightsee. In St. Louis, I left the convention center and walked to the main part of town. I walked up and down Main Street and through many of the stores. I then walked down to the Mississippi River and through the museum at the Gateway Arch.

After eating lunch in a floating restaurant, I walked to the old courthouse, scene of the famous Dred Scott case. Afterwards, I walked on to Busch Field, home of the St. Louis Cardinals.

The lady in the gift shop said I should take the walking tour of the stadium. So, with a speaker box around my neck to the left, a tape recorder around my neck to the right, and my camera hung around my neck to the front, I started on the walking tour.

The lady said I would hear the sound of a cardinal and then a voice would tell me which direction to take for the next stop on the tour. I never did get to the right place with the tape. After about an hour of walking and almost choking to death with the things hanging around my neck, I finally made it back to the gift shop.

I asked the lady if she would call me a cab. "Cabs only come to the stadium when there is a game," she said. "Where can I catch one?"

I asked. She told me to go up the street two blocks to a certain hotel and I would find a cab stand. I didn't think I could walk another two blocks, but I did. I asked the first cab driver I saw if his cab was available. "Get in," he said.

"Take me to the Convention Center Hotel," I said. The driver turned and looked at me with a puzzled look. He pointed out the back window and asked, "That hotel right there?"

Looking out the window, I could see my hotel about one block away. "It sure looks like it to me," I replied.

"You want me to take you there?" he asked.

"If you are for hire, I do," I said.

He turned the cab around and drove me to my hotel. "How much do I owe you?" I asked.

"Every bit of a dollar," he answered.

"And well worth it," I replied.

One of the most unforgettable characters was a taxi driver in Dallas. We had flown into the Dallas-Fort Worth Airport. A taxi ride from there into Dallas is about $16.

When we got into the cab, I noticed a trumpet lying in the front seat. "You play the trumpet?" I asked.

"Yes," he said, "in the band at the Assembly of God church where I attend. I keep it in my cab and practice with the music on the radio when I have time."

He asked what business we were in. I told him we were Southern Baptist preachers coming to a convention. When I said that, he reached over and turned the meter off.

"Why did you do that?" I asked.

"I never charge preachers," he said.

I reminded him that it was a $16 fare from the airport to downtown.

"Look," he said, "the only thing I can do in church is play in the band. I don't have the ability to teach and preach, but I can help God's preachers. So don't deprive me of my chance. Just pray for me."

Many times I have been reminded of the taxi driver in Dallas. I ask God to bless him and to make us preachers worthy of his trust.

## The Little Gold Pin

My wife received a phone call from her cousin, telling her that she had a gift for her. She wanted to place the gift in my wife's hand. She did not want to risk sending it through the mail.

We agreed to meet her one day for lunch. We drove the 60 miles to Greenville, discussing the possibilities of what the gift might be.

Cousin Mary Jane held us in suspense until after we had ordered our meals from the waiter. She then reached down into her large purse and took out a little white box with a rubber band around it.

She placed the little white box into my wife's hand and said, "I want to give you one of my most precious keepsakes that I have." My wife opened the box and found a little gold bar pin. Our cousin, settling back into her chair and sipping her coffee, said, "Now I want to tell you the story of that little gold pin."

The story she told began during the American Civil War. General William T. Sherman had led the Union troops in the siege of Atlanta from May 1 to September 8, 1864. After the fall of Atlanta, Sherman marched his troops to Savannah. They completed the now-famous "March to the Sea" in 24 days. They had marched some 300 miles. Savannah fell to Sherman on December 21, 1864. With these victories behind him, Sherman was ready to march toward Richmond. In the spring of 1865, he marched northward through the Carolinas. It was a march of destruction and pilferage.

While the main body of troops marched together, there were little bands of foragers that covered the countryside, plundering farms and homes. They were getting supplies for the Union Army. One of these little bands came to the farm of my wife's great-great-grandparents, John and Lucinda Norris. My wife's great-great-grandfather had been wounded in battle and was not at home when the "Yankees" came. The troops raided the farm, killing the livestock and burning the crops and buildings. While raiding the house, they ripped a pair of amethyst earrings from great-great-grandmother Lucinda's ears. She bore the scars for the rest of her life.

Fearing that they might be killed, she wrapped a shawl about herself and fled with her children into the fields. She was pregnant at the time, and the shock of the events rushed on the time for her to give birth. Her children made a bed of cornstalks for her in a gully in the field. Following the mother's instructions, an 11-year-old daughter named Jane and a younger brother helped their mother give birth to twin daughters.

One thing the foragers had failed to get in their plundering was the little gold pin that Great-Great-Grandmother wore on the collar of her dress. It had been hidden by the shawl.

Our cousin told us that before great-great-grandmother Lucinda died, she gave the little pin to her oldest daughter Jane. Before great-grandmother Jane died, she gave the pin to our cousin Mary Jane, who is now in her seventies.

And now she had placed the little gold pin in my wife Mary Jane's hands. There it will remain as a priceless family heirloom.

# My Electric Train

I grew up poor, but so did everybody on the street where I lived. We made most of our toys from scraps and leftover things. Our Romper-Stompers were made from empty oil cans and pieces of rope. Our trucks and cars were made from two-by-fours with empty thread spools for the wheels.

Christmas was a special time for us. It was the one time each year when we got a store-bought toy. We did not get a lot of things, but we did get a new toy each Christmas.

One Christmas was very special to us boys. My dad's boss man, Mr. Tripp, collected electric trains. He did not have any children. He would get my brother and me and take us to his house on Saturdays and let us run his trains. One whole room of his house was full of electric trains.

On this special Christmas Eve, we heard the door bell ring after we boys had gone to bed. We just knew that it was Santa Claus. (He couldn't come down the chimney because we had a fire in the fireplace.) We got out of bed and slipped up the hall. The door from the hall to the living room was shut. We peeped through the keyhole to see Santa. Instead, we saw Daddy's boss man putting one of his electric trains under our tree. Well, we could hardly go back to sleep. We wanted to play with our very own electric train.

That was one of the best Christmas gifts we ever received. That was Mr. Tripp's gift to us. I still have that train. I've had it for more than 40 years. Sometimes my son and I put the old train together and just watch it run again.

# What's It Like to Be a Paperboy?

What's it like to be a paperboy? My son asked me that question recently. It brought to mind those days when I was a carrier for The Greenville News-Piedmont.

My first route was a Piedmont route in downtown Greenville. I rode the city bus from Parker High School to the News-Piedmont building on South Main Street. My route ran through the businesses on the left side of Main Street.

I got to meet many interesting people on that route. One of those that I remember most was a lawyer named W.G. Sirrine. His office

was in the old Masonic Temple on South Main. He found out
through his secretary that I wanted to go to the Parker band camp. I
was not going because I could not afford the cost. One day his secretary said that he wanted to see me. He questioned me about the camp,
and then took a check from his desk drawer and gave it to me. The
check was the exact amount of the cost of the camp. I ran the rest of
the way around my route so that I could get home and tell my parents
the good news. Because I got to go to band camp that year, I made the
band.

My second route was a Greenville News route in the City View
community. Now, the early morning darkness can be a little scary. The
report was out that a mountain lion was stalking the Union Bleachery
community. The paper carried the story. The sheriff's department had
organized a search. Many people had reported signs of the lion's exis-
tence.

City View and Union Bleachery are not that far apart. And those
mornings seemed extra dark. The only comfort that I had was two
huge boxer bulldogs that followed me around my route.

One morning seemed to be just too dark and too quiet. To add to
my dismay, the boxer bulls failed to show up. I had only gone a few
streets when I heard it—the ear-piercing howl of the mountain lion.
It caused my heart to leap up into my throat.

I began to run and throw papers at the same time. The faster I ran,
the louder the cry of the lion. I could feel the beast breathing down
my back. A cold sweat ran across my face. At the end of one street, I
saw a tractor-trailer truck parked. I thought that if I could make that
truck, I could get away from the lion.

Just as I leaped for the truck, I met my lion face-to-face. With one
more loud howl, the blasted air starter on that diesel motor all but
scared me to death. I haven't cared too much for trucks like that since.

One other experience had a lasting effect on me. One of my cus-

tomers had a cabinet shop. I spent a good bit of time there each time I went by to collect. I watched him as he worked, and I suppose I asked him a thousand questions about cabinet work. He was always kind and patient with me.

He had problems that sometimes got the best of him. One Saturday when I went by to collect, I found him sitting on a work bench, crying. He looked up at me and asked, "Boy, can you pray?"

I said, "I think so."

"Then pray for me now." So we got down on our knees in the sawdust and I prayed, as well as I could, for my friend.

That was the first time that I was asked to pray for someone. As a minister, I am asked to do that many times. But I don't think I will ever forget the first time.

What's it like to be a paperboy? It's an experience that you will never forget.

## Bring Them In

Our church is located in the western part of South Carolina.

We are not very far from the Georgia state line. Because of this, many of our church members are natives of Georgia.

Our pianist's youngest son thought it nice recently when we sang a song about Georgia in the Sunday morning service. When asked which song he had made reference to, he replied, "You know, 'Bring Them In'!"

"How is that song about Georgia?" his mother asked.

"Well," he answered, "we sang, 'We shall come to Georgia, bringing in the peas'!"

## The Rains Came Down

It was one of those occasions when the worship service and the weather seemed to be on a collision course. It began to rain just as the service started.

Since the weather had been dry for weeks, the first hymn selected by our music director seemed fine. Everyone joined in singing "There Shall Be Showers of Blessing."

As the service continued, so did the rain, and everyone smiled as the hymn, "Higher Ground," was announced as the second hymn.

Then, the director blushed and the people began to laugh as "Throw Out the Lifeline" was announced as our final hymn.

# These I Remember

There are many things that helped shape the memory of childhood. Each one of them could be a story in itself. I plan only to mention some of them that I remember. You can probably remember a lot more than these. If so, write down your memories and share them.

I remember the basketball goal on the chinaberry tree made from a barrel hoop.

I remember making transfers from the color Sunday comics by using a yellow crayon and notebook paper.

I remember my pet chicken pecking a chicken pox off of my chin.

I remember coming home from school on a cold day and finding a pot of hot cornmeal mush on the stove.

I remember the smell of yeast bread rising on the hearth behind the Warm Morning stove in the dining room.

I remember eating hot dogs in homemade yeast rolls.

I remember homemade waffles and breakfast bacon on Sunday mornings.

I remember polishing everybody's shoes on Saturday night so that they would look good on Sunday.

I remember the Saturday night bath in the No. 3 tin tub.

I remember when we got our first bathtub. It had cold running water.

I remember the little white Tom's candy cabinet at Mr. Gossett's Esso station.

I remember the nail keg that Uncle Verner Brown gave me to play with. I still have a nail keg.

I remember hiding behind the banisters on the front porch during the air-raid warnings during World War II.

I remember riding the electric trolley to town on Friday nights.

I remember Daddy buying us Spanish peanuts, chocolate drops,

and Fig Newtons at Woolworth's candy counter.

I remember using Mama's stockings for Christmas stockings and finding them stretching from the mantle to the floor, filled with candy, fruit and nuts.

I remember the nightcaps made from Mama's old stockings.

I remember the plaster ceiling falling on the bed during the night.

I remember the Saturday nights when Uncle Benton and his boys came over to watch Texas wrestling on TV.

I remember Mama's jonquils blooming through the snow and the Easter roses that grew in the corner of the front yard.

I remember bringing in the buckets of coal so that we could build fires in the open fireplaces.

I remember helping to cut up the fruit for Mama's fruitcakes.

I remember helping taste the first white divinity candy.

I remember parking cars in the front yard to make enough money to go to the Parker football games.

I remember the Blankenships' parrot calling "Sammy" when I went by on my way to school.

I remember Mrs. Oney Martin's two Pekingese dogs that looked like her.

I remember waiting for Aunt Eade to come home so that I could earn a nickel crawling through the window to unlock the door which she had locked and left the key inside.

I remember riding the P&N to Cheddar to see Uncle Alton and Aunt Ginney.

I remember Daddy chasing Wilma around the house with a broom handle and two deacons from the church were next door at the Esso station, buying gas.

I remember the whistle blowing each morning at the little mill while I was delivering papers.

I remember the church chimes playing each Sunday morning.

I remember soaking my foot in kerosene oil after stepping on a rusty nail.

I remember eating orange slice candy after taking castor oil.

I remember the back yard when it didn't have grass on it.

# "Minister's Desk"

*The following columns are a sampling of the popular spiritual life lessons that Horace Sims wrote for his hometown paper, the Greenwood Index-Journal.*

## A Little Bird Told Me So

"Times are real bad," a friend said to me the other day. "So many people out of work... just don't know what we're gonna do."

I overheard a lady at the grocery store say, "We may all be starving before this thing's over." And when my wife told me what a pair of jeans cost, I thought my friend was right—times are real bad.

Now, some who are troubled about these difficult days begin to wonder if God really cares. Their minds are filled with doubt about the future. Where will they get food and shelter and clothes?

Well, let me tell you about what I saw. There was a large bush just outside my bedroom window. I started to cut it down when I made a discovery. I found a little nest full of eggs, nestled in one of the upper branches, so I left the bush alone and began to keep an eye on the nest.

I watched as the wind blew and the rains fell. The little nest stayed secure. No matter how hard the storm, it could not dislodge the nest

*Horace B. Sims*

from the bush.

Finally, the eggs hatched, and the nest was filled with little birds. The were unable to care for themselves, but the mother was there with bits of food to feed them.

Soon they began to grow and put on feathers. One day they were big enough to fly. Dressed in all of their feathered finery, they flew off in the clear blue sky, another testimony of God's care.

In the Sermon on the Mount, Jesus talked about the birds. He said: "Look at the birds of the air; they do not sow or reap or store away in barns, and yet your heavenly Father feeds them. Are you not much more valuable than they? So don't worry, saying, 'What shall we eat?' or 'What shall we drink?' or 'What shall we wear?'"

Does God care for you? Will God take care of you? Can you trust God to meet your needs in these "bad" times?

Yes, you can! I know. A little bird told me so.

## Putting on a New Uniform

A few nights ago, I, along with several hundred more people, got to see the Greenwood High School band march in its new uniforms for the first time. It was a splendid sight.

The band is something that all of Greenwood can and should be proud of. It has placed high in the state band contest for several years. That is an honor to our city.

My love for marching bands goes way back. I marched in the Parker High School band for five years. I later marched in the Furman University ROTC band.

I remember when I got my first band uniform. It had been worn by several bandsmen before me and had some frayed places on it. It was still the best looking set of clothes I had ever worn.

Each year the senior band members would get new uniforms. This was the way our band had of replacing old uniforms. I could hardly wait for my senior year to come. I'd had only one suit in my life. It was a black one from the O.P.O. store, but it was nothing to compare to a new band uniform.

The day finally came when the rising seniors were to be fitted for new uniforms. The expectation of wearing a new uniform kept me excited all summer.

We dressed in our uniforms for the first football game of the season. I felt ten feet tall as I strutted down Woodside Avenue to the football field that night. I just knew every eye in the stadium was on me and my band uniform.

The Apostle Paul talked about putting on new clothes. He said we were to put on the new man. The apostle was really saying, "Put on your new uniform." By faith in Jesus Christ, this is possible. The new birth is simply laying aside the old, frayed and torn way of life and putting on the new.

The Christian experience is available to all who would want to live a new life. Come along with me and put on your new uniforms.

## The Gift of His Prayer

I was born and reared in the city. I have always lived in town. City life had many advantages. The ice man delivered ice to our front door for the ice box. The trash truck came by to collect our trash. The electric trolley came right by our house. For a token and a transfer, you could ride all over town. Our house had running water and inside plumbing and a door bell.

Even though I enjoyed city life, there was always something fascinating about the country. Each summer, we would go to the country to spend some time with our aunts and uncles. One aunt and uncle lived in a big white house on top of a hill. They called it Pea Ridge. It had a big kitchen with a large open fireplace.

My aunt loved to cook in that fireplace. She would hang pots of green beans with ham hocks and pots of turnip greens on the hooks over the fire. She put cornbread and biscuits in the Dutch ovens in the coals on the hearth. You have never really eaten until you eat food cooked like that.

Now, my aunt and uncle were devoted Christians. They were members of the Wesleyan Church. They took their faith seriously. One of the things I remember most about those summer visits were Uncle Cephas' prayers. Each night before we went to bed, he would call us all to the kitchen for prayer. He prayed fervently for all the family. He prayed for his neighbors and their needs. He prayed for his church and his pastor. It seemed like those prayers would last an hour.

Though they were long, I knew that somehow they were real. I sensed that my uncle was really talking to God.

Down through the years, I, too, have come to appreciate the gift of prayer. What a wonderful thing it is that God has given us. He has given an open channel to heaven itself.

Prayer takes many forms. There are prayers of thanksgiving, when we simply thank God for all that He has done for us. There are prayers of intercession, when we pray for others. And there are prayers of petition, when we ask God to meet our own needs.

Whatever your prayer, God has promised to hear and answer from heaven. Have you used the gift of prayer today? Why not? It could be the solution to all your problems.

Paul, the apostle, said, "Pray without ceasing." When you do, your life will be richer.

## Taking Time to Look at Life

I was a carrier for the Greenville Piedmont in downtown Greenville when I was in the seventh grade. Since we lived in City View, I had to ride the electric trolley to town each day.

I always had an argument with the trolley driver over whether I could use a student ticket to go to work. He always gave in, and I rode to town on a ticket.

There were a lot of interesting people on that route. I served a good many lawyers and real estate men. I got to know most of the store managers and clerks.

Downtown Greenville was exciting in those days. You got to see all the parades, and the fire trucks were constantly going up and down Main Street.

Woolworth's and Silver's always had popcorn and peanut machines in front of their stores, filling the air with tempting odors. I could usually sneak a sample from one or the other, and I wasn't above trading an evening paper for a bag of peanuts.

Most of the time you could hear a good sermon from one of the street preachers. There was one regular preacher who preached in front of Silver's. Even though I didn't have time to listen to all of his sermons, I usually heard a little of them.

One group that I remember well were the street beggars. One was blind and sold pencils. Another wore heavy leather pads on his knees and crawled everywhere he went. One man had no legs at all. He sat in a wheelchair and sold sewing needles.

Somehow these people seemed to illustrate life as it really is. The preacher preaching, the beggars begging, and all around them people rushing to and fro without time to take note of them.

How nice it would be if we would take time to look at life from all sides, and, when we had looked, then take time to thank God for all He has given us.

# A Rose Is a Rose

My father's hobby was growing roses. Beginning in May, our yard would be ablaze with the various colors of roses. The fence down one side of our lot would look like a wall of red.

In the front yard, there was a very unusual rose. It was called an Easter rose. It seemed to always bloom at Easter. So many people asked to get a clipping root that the bush just disappeared.

Dad bought one bush that was a new variety. To make it strong, the new variety had been grafted to the older roots of another type of rose. The new variety died, and the older roots began to grow. They produced a large bush that had little talisman buds. The were just about the most beautiful in the entire garden.

Shakespeare said, "A rose is a rose, and by any other name would smell the same." He was right. Roses have a distinct scent all their own. With slight variation, they all smell the same.

You might say they are much like Christians. Christians are not all white, nor are they all black or any other color. They are not all rich or all poor, all educated or all ignorant.

Christians come in all sizes, colors and nationalities. They may speak different languages and eat different foods. They may be Baptist, Methodist, Lutheran, Presbyterian, Pentecostal or a hundred other varieties. But, in essence, they are all the same.

Christians are those people who have committed themselves to Jesus Christ and have accepted Him as their Lord and Savior. Just as the roses are one distinct family of flowers, so are Christians the family of God.

## Making Use of Reflections

Crossing the lake one evening this week, I saw the reflection of the sunset. It was a double view of the many beautiful colors, and I thought how necessary reflections are to our lives.

How many of us would start the day without seeing our reflection in a mirror? It helps us to know if our hair is combed or if our tie is straight. Consider the dismay of the ladies without a mirror to see how to apply makeup.

There are other types of reflection. The word can also mean "to meditate." This is reflection on one's life. This is most important at the beginning of a new year.

You should reflect on your failures of the past year. Let them become a lesson for the year to come. Someone said, "It is no shame to make a mistake, as long as you do not make the same mistake twice."

Learn from your mistakes. Determine not to make the same ones again. Know the reason for failure, and shun that reason this year.

You should also reflect on your successes. Were you really successful in something this past year? Then you should know why you had success. This reflection will give you the right motive for success again this year.

Your life itself can be a reflection. Your attitudes can reflect what you really are inwardly. A smile can reflect inner peace, while a frown can reflect a bad disposition. A kind word spoken reflects a compassionate person. Harsh words reflect a person who does not enjoy inward peace.

There is a special reflection reserved for the Christian person. A Christian's life should reflect the life of Christ. His love should be seen in our love. His peace should reflect in our countenance. His great compassion should reflect in the way that we treat other people.

There is a hymn that challenges us to have this reflection of Jesus in our lives:

*While passing through this world of sin*
*And others your life shall view*
*Be pure and clean without, within,*
*Let others see Jesus in you.*

## Life Is Worth Living

There are times when we think life is really not worth living. But it may be that we are looking for the wrong things. There are some things that will add joy to the day. They will make life worth living if you look for them.

Hear the laughter of a child. Listen to that child ask questions from innocence and wish that you were there. I was reminded of that recently when my son asked, "Daddy, what is worry?"

Help someone with their burdens. Get your eyes off yourself. This help may be costly, or it could just be a warm smile and a kind word. It could just be a listening ear.

Be honest with everyone. Whether you gain or lose, above all, be honest. Integrity is one of the missing virtues of our day. If you lose your integrity, you lose everything.

Read something worthwhile each day. Someone once said: "The man who does not read is no better than the man who cannot read."

Read a chapter from the Bible each day. It will give you help with the day's problems.

Listen to a little good music. Experience the calmness that it can give. When King Saul had fits of madness, David was summoned to play for the king on his harp. The music would calm the mad mind of the king. Sometimes, in the mad rush of the day, we need to hear that type of music.

Commune with God each day. Start each day with a talk with your heavenly Father. Listen for Him to speak to you throughout the day. Hear Him in the child's laughter. Hear Him in the song of the birds. See Him in the colors of the leaves and the flowers. Feel him in the winds that blow about you. Know Him in that still, small voice that speaks deep within you. If you look for the right things, life is worth living each day. Give it another try.

*Life is worth living if you really try,*
*If you don't let good things pass you by.*
*Like the laughter of a child*
*Playing a melody sweet,*
*Or the help you give,*
*Making someone's day complete.*
*Like the colors of autumn*
*Making God seem so near,*
*Or the book that you read,*
*And the music you hear,*
*And if through the day*
*You talk to God above*
*He'll answer from heaven*
*And fill you with love.*

# Accepting the Best Things

I attended elementary school at the City View Elementary School in Greenville. It was the same school that my father had attended as a boy.

On a cold winter night, many years ago, I stood and watched the old school burn. It had been used as a warehouse for several years. Many memories went through my mind as I watched the flames devour that building.

One memory that still lingers is that of the lunch wagon. It was a large cart that was rolled about on bicycle-type wheels. It was much like a portable steam table. The wagon was brought from the school kitchen to our classrooms, where we were served our meals.

You may not believe this, but I hated to see that thing coming. I literally dreaded for lunch time to come. It seemed that we would have white corn hominy, big dry limas, asparagus or rice pudding every day. As a boy, I totally disliked all those foods. My favorite food was a hot dog, and we never got them for school lunch.

Now, if you didn't eat all of your food, you would get the palm of your hand rapped with a Coca-Cola ruler. The palms of my hands stayed sore all the time.

It was some years later that I understood about the nutritional value of food. The teacher would say, "You must eat all of your food. It's good for you." But I was hard to convince.

I have found that the things that are best for us in life are not the most enjoyable at the moment. Some people view the Christian life this way. They resent the idea of commitment. Some say that the Christian life is full of negative prohibitions. Like the food, they would rather have something more enjoyable. We know, however, that nutritional food develops healthy bodies.

Any negative prohibitions in the Christian life are only steps to a more positive way of life. The Christian life is the only way that I know to produce total wholeness of life. I invite you to join me in the way.

## Light at the End of the Tunnel

I have been speaking at a church in Oconee County this week. It is a lovely part of the state, especially in the fall.

One of the more famous attractions there is the Stumphouse Mountain Tunnel. It has been a popular attraction for over 100 years. The tunnel was to be a part of the old Blue Ridge Railroad. The railroad was to run from Charleston to Cincinnati, Ohio. It would have connected South Carolina to the West.

The work on the tunnel was begun in 1856. It was to be 5,863 feet long through solid granite. By 1859, the tunnel had reached a

length of over 1,600 feet. The company doing the work began to have financial problems and could not continue. The Civil War happened, and the idea of the railroad died. The tunnel has remained unfinished ever since.

A few years ago, I visited the tunnel for the first time. I took a small lantern and began to walk back into the darkness. After a while, I had gone so far into the tunnel that the darkness became foreboding. The light from my small lantern did not seem as bright as when I started into the tunnel.

For a moment, I almost panicked. I could feel the darkness closing in on me. Then I remembered to turn and look in the other direction. Off in the distance, I could see the opening of the tunnel. It seemed to be so small, but it was my ray of hope. I headed for that light and was soon back out in the open daylight.

Sometimes life seems like a dark tunnel. Many things can cause it to be so. Our sins, troubles and sorrows can all add to the darkness.

Just when the darkness seems most threatening, we can find the light to lead us out. If we look by faith to Jesus Christ, we will see the light at the end of the tunnel. It may seem like a faint ray at first, but, as our faith grows, the light will become brighter.

The Apostle John said: "In Him was life; and the life was the light of men. And the light shineth in darkness; and the darkness could not overcome it."

## An Exciting, Fulfilling Journey

While visiting an antique shop recently, I saw a little advertising blotter that brought back memories. It was an advertisement for the P&N Railroad. The P&N was known as the "Great Electric System of the South." It ran from Charlotte, North Carolina, to Greenwood, South Carolina.

The little blotter carried a slogan which read, "Ride with a Smile for a Penny a Mile." Tickets actually cost one cent for each mile you rode.

The P&N tracks crossed the street that I lived on as a boy. We would occasionally ride the train to visit some of our relatives. The trip from Greenville to Cheddar would cost about 25 cents each.

Dad would stand by the tracks, and, as the train came into sight, he would start to flag it with his handkerchief. The old electric engine would screech to a stop. The conductor would hop off the passenger car and yell, "If you're going with me, get on! I ain't got all day!"

The trip was short, and only cost a family of five $1.25, but to a boy it was an exciting journey.

The old train doesn't run anymore, but there is a way to travel through life that is even more exciting than it was. That way is the Christian way of life. The ticket for this way has already been paid. In His atoning sacrifice, our Lord has paid the price of the way.

The trip will be demanding. It will demand of us time, talent, service and commitment. This trip will not only be exciting, but fulfilling. Come along, join me in the way.

## Getting Excited About Christmas

I sat in one of the state's large shopping malls last week and watched thousands of shoppers rushing by. Their arms were heavy laden with Christmas gifts.

I sat near where Santa Claus was. The children were in an endless line, hoping to get to talk to the jolly old fellow. So much excitement filled their faces, I started to get in line myself.

As I watched them, I thought back to my childhood and remembered how excited we got at Christmas time. We put our tree up right after Thanksgiving. We could hardly wait for the time to come when we would go to the woods to get our tree.

Mama had her fruitcakes baked and stored away. Each day we

would do something to get ready for the big day. We cleaned the house and polished all the furniture and the mantles with Old English furniture oil. We decorated everything that could be decorated.

On Friday nights we would ride the electric trolley downtown to go Christmas shopping. We always started at Main and Washington in downtown Greenville. That's where the dime stores were. The streets were all ablaze with strands of Christmas lights. The Salvation Army lassies were ringing their bells, and the stores were all playing Christmas music.

The most exciting time of all was when we got to see Santa Claus. We told him what we would like to get for Christmas, and he promised to bring it if we would be good. Nobody was ever bad during December.

The excitement grew until the big day finally arrived. Santa Claus had come and brought us the things we had hoped for. It really didn't matter that, for some reason, he had forgotten one or two things. We knew he would bring them next year.

Christmas has always been an exciting time. It is a day that marks the birth of Jesus Christ. This was one of the most looked-for events in history. The people in Old Testament times had looked for the promised Messiah for years. Their prophets had written about the coming event. The talk of it was constantly on their lips.

The night finally came. It was heralded by angels from heaven. Shepherds and kings alike came to honor Him. This is the true meaning of Christmas, and it is exciting good news.

"Unto us a child is born, unto us a son is given."

## She Sang a Song of Faith

"We are in hard times again," a friend said to me the other day, "and a lot of young people don't know anything about hard times."

That statement caused me to think back to the days when I was a boy. I suppose it was "hard times" for us, but we sure enjoyed those times.

Our house had cold running water. Our bathtub was a No. 3 wash tub. Boy, was that thing cold on a winter night. We would sit it in front of the old Warm Morning heater so it could warm up before we got in.

Our house was not underpinned. When the cold winter winds would blow, the old linoleum rugs would hum on the floor, and the curtains would stand out from the windows. We slept under so many quilts that we woke up tired from holding them up all night.

We walked about a mile to school each day. When we got home on those cold days, Mama would have us a good hot snack ready. She would have a pot of hot cornmeal mush on the stove. Sometimes she would even have some fatback fried to go with it. Now, that wasn't Little Debbies or Twinkies, but it sure was good to cold children. I'm getting hungry just thinking about it.

The thing that really remains in my mind from those days was Mama's faith. When we came into the house, we could hear Mama singing in the kitchen. She always sang the same song:

*What a friend we have in Jesus,*
*All our sins and griefs to bear!*
*What a privilege to carry*
*Everything to God in prayer!*
*Oh, what peace we often forfeit,*
*Oh, what needless pain we bear,*
*All because we do not carry*
*Everything to God in prayer!*

That song was a song of faith, and when we heard it coming from the kitchen, we knew that everything was all right.

In hard times, as well as in good times, we need to exercise our faith. Faith is trust in God to take care of us. The Apostle Paul said: "My God shall supply all your needs by His riches in Glory."

Yes, it is "hard times" for many people. Some are out of work and face many hard decisions. We are being forced to live a lifestyle that many find difficult. Now is the time to sing a song of faith. God has never failed you, and He won't now. Exercise your faith, and enjoy life.

# SECTION THREE

# Poems

*From his personal collection, these poems faithfully convey Horace Sims' deepest feelings about the things that mattered most to him: his God, his family and his memories of home.*

# A Place Called Home

It was just an old frame house standing by the road,
　　But, to us, it was a place to call home;
And still we love to come and meet there,
　　No matter how far away we may roam.

It had five rooms, a big porch, and one semi-bath,
　　And it gave shelter to two parents, three boys, and a girl.
It lacked underpinning, but it had plaster walls,
　　And the linoleum hummed when winter winds would whirl.

It was complete with cold running water and electric lights;
　　And the dining room even had a Warm Morning heater.
The cook stove was fueled by kerosene oil,
　　And we bathed in a tin tub—what could be neater?

Christmas was always a happy time there,
　　For in the kitchen could be found ham, turkey and cake;
And our relatives came pouring in by droves
　　To eat and laugh and give the old place a shake.

Well, the days have come and the days have gone,
　　And the house that was home for Mom, Dad, Ronnie,
Tony, Wilma and me
Now bulges and groans and moans, for besides us,
　　There is Carroll, Rita, Jane, Ruby, Lynne, Kay, Sonya,
　　Stacy, Bryant, Rhonda ... and Thee.

# Mother

Today is hers, her very own day
   And I wish to thank her in a special way.
For all her tender loving care
   Has in my life left its mark there.

She made do with what she had
   And never let us know if things were bad.
She kept our clothes mended and clean
   And loved us even when we were mean.

Our home was never a sparkling mansion
   But for a happier place, it couldn't be outdone.
For when we came home feeling sad and low
   Her singing in the kitchen added a needed glow.

And our lives were pointed in the right direction
   Even though it sometimes took a little correction.
So on this special day, I wish to confer
   My deepest love and affection on Mother.

# Dad

He may be quiet and little known,
But he worked hard to have something of his own.
You may never have heard his name
But there are some who proclaim his fame.

For when there were hungry children to be fed,
He was the one who worked to buy them bread.
And when clothes were needed, he was willing to pay
So that we did not go without for even a day.

Even though a mansion was beyond his fold,
He provided a home that kept us out of the cold.
And we played and sang and worked some, too.
For in a family of six, there was always something to do.

Well, he saw us through until we were grown,
And now we are married with homes of our own.
But this is his day, and for that I am glad
Just to be able to say, "We love you, Dad."

# Jane

A bachelor I'd be until I died,
  And the Lord knows I really tried.
Until I saw, sitting there, counting shirts,
  A girl to whom I would throw many flirts.

And before we had traveled many a mile,
  I found myself walking down the aisle.
I was twenty-eight and poorly paid,
  But working together, our home we made.

It wasn't much, four rooms and all,
  But we soon had furniture wall to wall.
Then into our midst God did give
  A newborn daughter to come and live.

With my bride of little more than a year,
  We moved off to Columbia with little fear.
We had committed our lives to preaching the Word,
  And we had to go where we could be heard.

In my calling, many lonely hours I would've spent
  Had it not been for my wife, a gift God sent.
Not only does she cook and wash and mend,
  She brings real joy to the life we spend.

From her many experiences as a preacher's kid,
  She coaxes me on when I would have hid.
Then to our life she brought another joy
  When she made me the father of a baby boy.

No matter where in life we may roam,
    She will always make ours a happy home;
And whether over distant mountain or plain,
    I thank God every day for a wife named Jane.


# My Boy

What could give a man more joy
    Than to be the father of a little boy?
With eyes so big and clear and bright,
    You know that someday they'll be a girl's delight.

Oh, he may be filled with mischief and trouble,
    But way down deep, he'll cause you to bubble.
He'll ask a thousand questions about how and why;
    Some you can't answer, but still you'll try.

In his mind's eye, you reign as king,
    And to keep that image, you'll do anything.
He'll taunt you and tease you just for fun,
    Then when you try, he'll turn and run.

You've trained him well, you're prone to confess,
    And then you'll find his room in a terrible mess.
At times, the noise sounds like a full-blown twister;
    That's when he's fighting with his older sister.

His laughter, to you, is like a bird that sings
    And you thank God for the happiness he brings.
So with his every wish, you'll be compliant,
    Especially so when the boy's name is Bryant.

*Horace B. Sims*

# My Girl

Is there anything in the world
    Like being the father of a girl?
One who is so prissy and prancy,
    A little bit sissy and a good bit fancy.

She puts polish on her fingers and toes,
    And sometimes powders the end of her nose.
She will wear a frilly dress, too,
    But prefers pants if they will do.

In a tub of bubbles, she usually soaks,
    But forgets to give her hair a hundred strokes.
She leaves for school in such a tizzy
    It often leaves me just a little dizzy.

When on a paper, she makes a good grade,
    Around the house she loves to parade.
But when bad, she is in such gloom,
    She often goes and sulks in her room.

There is one thing for which she wishes:
    That is to never be asked to do the dishes.
While she has absolutely no use for a broom,
    She will occasionally straighten her room.

But none of these things are really a bother,
    Especially when she says, "I love you, Father."
And to my Heavenly Father will my praise be
    For He gave me a sweet daughter named Stacy.


# Wilma

'Twas on a cold January night when I was born,
    And to my sister that was as bad as a thorn.
That she really wanted a baby sister was true,
    And news of a baby brother just would not do.

Across the street she ran in a mad flurry;
    But I was her new brother and I didn't worry,
For through the years she would come to realize
    That having baby brothers was no real surprise.

She was the prettiest girl our daddy ever had;
    A saying that most of the time made her mad.
From her first job, she bought a television set,
    And her brothers' approval she did quickly get.

She soon grew up and began dating boys and all,
    And finally married a low-lander, lean and tall.
He had felt called to lead a preacher's life,
    And our sister wound up being a preacher's wife.

She later became mother of two pretty girls,
    Who usually left their uncles spinning in swirls.
And always at her table you could find
    A meal to almost put you out of your mind.

As we come together to celebrate this day,
    May we join our hearts and earnestly pray
That our Lord deliver us from many a dilemma
    And help us always remember our sister, Wilma.

## Uncle Benton Davis' Farm

How well I remember Uncle Benton Davis' farm,
    For, to a city boy, it was a place full of charm.
It seems like such a long, long time ago,
    But memories of that place still make my heart glow.

You see, as a city boy I was born and bred,
    And I suppose I'll be that until I'm dead.
But many were the good times at that farm I spent,
    And to go there in the summer was a big event.

The beds always had a pleasant country smell,
    And I loved to help draw buckets of water from the well.
The aroma I smelled as day was first dawning
    Came from the wood cook stove where Aunt Clara was
cooking.

*Whistling at Snakes*

After breakfast, there were many chores to be done,
    And feeding cows and pigs, to a city boy, was really fun.
And when the sun got too hot, off we would streak
    Across the pasture to swim in old Six Mile Creek.
Well, time has divided us by many long miles,
    But the times we had there are remembered with smiles.
And though time and place may forever keep us apart,
    I'll always remember Uncle Benton Davis' farm in my heart.

# Thirty-Nine

Life is a funny thing to me;
    I was sure I'd die by thirty-three.
Such a fate just was not mine,
    So now I'm a little past thirty-nine.

Well, my hair has a silver lining,
    And on top my dome is shining.
Though the years have added to my girth,
    It was really mine from my birth.

Even though it gives no real pleasure,
    Pills do control my blood pressure,
And medicated powder I must put
    On my feet for athlete's foot.

I may even live to seventy-two,
    Provided I don't catch the flu,
And if I do, I may even shout,
    Only if it doesn't hurt my gout.

# Old Rebel

(For Harold Bryson, upon the loss of his dog, Rebel.)

He shared the woe
    Of broken hearts,
Of pain, of grief
    When one departs.

Of storm-tossed nights,
    Of sunless morrows,
Of flowing tears
    When a family sorrows.

He told of a search
    Of hours unending,
Of kindhearted friends
    When souls needed mending.

He told of days, of weeks,
    Of months slowly passing,
Of the mind's anguish
    When hope's not lasting.

And we all knew
    'Twas the work of the devil,
But, alas, we must say
    Farewell to old Rebel.

# Itis

I hear that your bronchitis
Has aggravated your tonsillitis
And that you even have laryngitis.

The news does, however, excite us
Just to learn that your arthritis
Has not yet aggravated your neuritis.

# Justice, Mercy, Grace

Justice! Oh no, oh no,
    Please don't let it be,
For my sins are dark and many
    And it cannot set me free.

Mercy! Oh, please dear Lord,
    Let it fall upon my ear:
"Your sins are forgiven
    And you need never fear."

Grace! Oh, hallelujah,
    The message from above
Has filled my heart with joy
    And bathed me in His love.

# Lasting Joy

Have your days been dark and dreary?
Have your burdens left you weary?
Have you longed for some light to see,
Or some friend to set you free?

Have you faced the world afraid?
Have life's trials left you dismayed?
Have your eyes been filled with tears,
And you are aging beyond your years?

Then one question I ask of you,
And from your heart, answer true:
Have you taken time to pray
And talked with the Lord today?

In Him you'll find sweet release,
In Him is comfort and peace.
Trust Him, His power employ,
He'll fill your heart with lasting joy.

*Horace B. Sims*

# A Prayer

My Heavenly Father from above,
    Let me feel the strength of your love.
When my heart is burdened with care,
    Let me know that you are there.
Dear Father, when my days are filled with strife,
    Help me to find in you peace for life.
And when my own way has brought me sorrow,
    Let me see in you a brighter tomorrow.
Then let me walk by faith each day,
    Trusting in you to lead me in the right way.
And when with life's battles I am done,
    Let me dwell in heaven with your dear Son.

# Sanctimonious

Sitting sanctimoniously in the sanctuary,
    Showing piety in the pew.
As cold in June as in January,
    Love's warmth found in but a few.

The world outside is crying;
    Sin is devouring like a flame.
Men all around us are dying,
    And our piety may be to blame.

The call for help is sounding;
    Lost souls look for one to come.
Their look may turn to longing,
    For the will to respond seems numb.

*Whistling at Snakes*

Will we leave them lost and weary,
    Not showing them life anew,
While sitting sanctimoniously in the sanctuary
    And showing piety in the pew?

# I Know That God Lives

When I hear the birds that sing
And see the flowers bloom in spring,
I know that God lives.

When I listen to a bubbling brook run
And feel the warm rays of the sun,
I know that God lives.

When I feel the warm summer rain
And smell the roses by the lane,
I know that God lives.

When I see the changing color of the leaves
And watch them fall with an autumn breeze,
I know that God lives.

When I feel the cold winter wind blow
And walk on paths covered with snow,
I know that God lives.

When I awake to a bright sunrise
And watch it set in a fiery demise,
I know that God lives.

When I, at night, kneel down to pray
And thank Him for this, another day,
I know that God lives.

When sin has filled my heart with sorrow
And He gives me hope of a better tomorrow,
I know that God lives.

# Just God and Me

I walked through the quiet woods today,
    All alone, just God and me.
And in His presence, I knelt to pray
    And sought earnestly His will to see.

I sat alone with God tonight
    And told Him all the burdens of my heart.
And in the darkness, I felt His might
    As He bid all my sins and fears depart.

I awoke this morning to feel God's love
    As warm as the morning rays of the sun.
And I heard Him call down from above
    To tell me that I am still His son.

# The First Cold Wind of Winter

The first cold wind of winter
    Blew its breath on us today,
And the sky heralded the arrival
    With blustery clouds of gray.

The icy breath brought a shiver
   To the naked limbs of the trees,
And made ocean-like waves
   In bending the straw to its knees.

The birds flying in pattern
   Seemed to fly a little faster,
And the old man walking the street
   Made each step a little quicker.

And, as the cold night began to settle,
   The sun gave one parting smile,
And somehow it just seemed to say
   That winter would be here for a while.

## The Morning Light

There's a quiet hush just before dawn,
   Quiet enough to hear all nature yawn.
Then comes the sound of a honeybee's wings,
   And off in the distance a mockingbird sings.
And the maple's cover of new green leaves
   Ripples softly in the early morning breeze,
While the flowers, bowed with a heavy dew,
   Begin to raise their heads for a glorious view.
At last the whole world seems to be humming,
   For out of darkness, Morning Light is coming.

And so it was with the souls of men;
   They were lost in a world full of sin.
Their heads were bowed, their hearts filled with fright
   As they sat in the lonesome darkness of night.

*Horace B. Sims*

And then there came through the prophet's voice
    A sound that would cause all men to rejoice.
For, like the flowers rising from the heavy dew,
    God was preparing to give men hope anew.
And now all their sad hearts could be singing,
    For new life, the Morning Light would be bringing.


## If I Had My Life to Live Over

If I had my life to live over,
    In a thousand different ways,
I'd make more use of each moment
    Of those quickly passing days;
I'd fill each second with wonder,
    Reaching for the distant star;
I'd set my course to sail onward,
    Gleaning from ports near and far;
I'd look for God in the flowers
    And see Him in every bloom;
I'd trust Him to fill the hours
    And never, never know gloom.
If I had my life to live over,
    I'd sing with the morning sun
And rest complete in the evening,
    Knowing my work had been done.

# Wonders I've Yet to See

In the quietness of the morning,
    I hear God speak to me,
And as day's light is dawning,
    He tells of wonders I've yet to see.

Sin as the darkness of night
    Has hid from me His face,
But up there in heaven's light,
    I'll sing the glory of His grace.

And when salvation's story's told,
    I'll lift my voice in thankful prayer,
And I'll walk along those streets of gold
    With all my loved ones waiting there.

And standing by the river, crystal clear,
    And eating from the Tree of Life,
My heart will know no pain or fear,
    Having left this world of strife.

In the shadows of the evening,
    God still speaks to me,
And my heart now has a longing
    For the wonders I've yet to see.

# Thomas Addison

"After reading Horace Sims' work and illustrating his stories, I'm only disappointed I couldn't collaborate with him," says illustrator and cartoonist Thomas Addison. "He reminds me of people I've grown up knowing, people who could find humor in any situation."

Addison's editorial cartoons have appeared in the Greenville News, the Anderson Independent-Mail and the Williamston Journal. His work has also been included in Pelican's "Best Editorial Cartoons of the Year."

Also a muralist, Addison has been commissioned to create historical works for communities across Upstate South Carolina. He recently was recruited by the town of Williamston to help in the formation of the newly created Williamston Cultural Arts Center, where he will serve as a member of its board of directors and head up the visual arts department.

Addison is a graduate of Western Carolina University and holds a master's degree from the University of South Carolina. He has taught art at Palmetto Middle School for 35 years.

For fun, he plays bass guitar and sings with his cousins in "Whitten City News," a variety band they formed about 40 years ago and have maintained under various names.

Addison and his wife, Roni, live in Pelzer, S.C., and worship at Powdersville Community Church, where Thomas assists with the music program. They are the parents of two children, Emily, 27, and Joseph, 17, and two granddaughters, Jada, 9, and Madison, 7.

(Updated 2013)

CPSIA information can be obtained
at www.ICGtesting.com
Printed in the USA
LVOW13s0123230617

539096LV00007B/291/P